WITHDRAWN

F R O N T
O F F I C E
OPERATIONS
and
AUDITING
WORKBOOK

F R O N T
O F F I C E
OPERATIONS
and
AUDITING
WORKBOOK

SECOND EDITION

Patrick J. Moreo
Oklahoma State University

Gail Sammons
University of Nevada Las Vegas

Jeff Beck
Oklahoma State University

Upper Saddle River, New Jersey 07458

Acquisitions Editor: Vernon R. Anthony
Production Editor: Marianne Hutchinson (Pine Tree Composition)
Production Liaison: Barbara Marttine Cappuccio
Director of Manufacturing and Production: Bruce Johnson
Managing Editor: Mary Carnis
Manufacturing Manager: Ed O'Dougherty
Art Director: Marianne Frasco
Cover Design Coordinator: Miguel Ortiz
Cover Designer: Amy Rosen
Marketing Manager: Ryan DeGrote
Editorial Assistant: Susan Kegler
Interior Design and Composition: Pine Tree Composition
Printing and Binding: Banta Harrisonburg

Prentice-Hall International (UK) Limited, *London*
Prentice-Hall of Australia Pty. Limited, *Sydney*
Prentice-Hall Canada Inc., *Toronto*
Prentice-Hall Hispanoamericana, S.A., *Mexico*
Prentice-Hall of India Private Limited, *New Delhi*
Prentice-Hall of Japan, Inc., *Tokyo*
Prentice-Hall Singapore Pte. Ltd.
Editora Prentice-Hall do Brasil, Ltda., *Rio de Janeiro*

10 9 8 7 6 5 4 3 2 1
ISBN 0-13-032493-0

Contents

Introduction

The goals of the *Front Office Operations and Auditing Workbook* have evolved over the years. It still begins with exercises to provide the user with a clearer insight into front office and guest accounting and operations. We accomplish this by having the student begin by performing a simple, manual audit of the guest accounts receivable, and then conclude with a computerized version of accomplishing the same thing. But, in order to provide tools for constant quality management and guest services, this latest edition contains an entirely new section on *operational auditing* in the front office and for guest services. Thus, the *Front Office Operations and Auditing Workbook* goes well beyond the traditional accounts receivable and income auditing.

While there are some hotels and inns that continue to use a hand transcript, the purpose here is not to necessarily teach students how to perform the manual night audit. Rather, we hope that the insight gained by seeing all the components of the night audit laid out before them would provide the users with the basic tools necessary to transfer their understanding to the many computer systems that have been and will be developed for performing the front office guest management accounting functions. These systems all change very rapidly in technical respects, but the underlying theories and principles remain the same: an audit and reconciliation of guests' bills with pertinent hotel records through standard bookkeeping and accounting techniques and the ability to track guest and room information with integration and ease.

In the first section, the student actually performs an entire day's front office transactions before beginning the audit itself. The preliminary front office guest management part of the exercise should put front office accounting operations into cycled perspective. For this reason, we strongly urge students to complete each problem in the order that the components of that problem appear—as though they were working in the front office from the morning on through the day and evening shifts and finally ending with the night audit itself.

The computer section of this book is designed to illustrate how front office operations flow from the manual foundation that we have laid in the context of an actual property management system. The goal is for the student to understand that, regardless of the techniques used, ultimately it is a clear *system* design that will lead to the goal of providing the guest with excellent, quick service and the hotel with accurate records. The student should have a clear understanding that indeed, with evolving computer driven systems, many of the checks and balances in original manual system become unnecessary because the possibility for posting error, for example, is eliminated and because information need be entered into the system only once. The *Workbook* reinforces theory with practice.

The new section on *front office operational auditing* can serve many purposes. At a minimum it gives students an overview of how the many functions that they read about in their textbook are actually applied and evaluated. Students can make even more extensive use of this section by using the Operational Audit or parts of it on field visits to hotels as a guide to understanding the hotel or even as a basis for doing a project in a hotel. It lends itself particularly well to group projects.

Preface

This *Front Office Operations and Auditing Workbook* is the result of experimentation in front office operations classes at the University of Nevada, Las Vegas, The Pennsylvania State University, New Mexico State University, and Oklahoma State University. The workbook evolved from over fifteen years of providing a technique for students to get a practical understanding of what they are learning in class. The exercises are intended as a reinforcement for the guest/room management as well as the accounting and night audit—"close of day" sections of lectures and textbooks in front office or hotel operations courses.

The *Front Office Operations and Auditing Workbook* is especially designed to be a companion to Drs. Jerome and Gary Vallen's *Check In—Check Out*, seventh edition. It is compatible with the corresponding sections of the major front office texts in use and under development and reinforces those sections of the texts with practical exercises.

The concept of using a practice set to reinforce classroom instruction is not new. As students at the then New York City Community College in the mid-1960s, we used similar approaches under the direction of Professor Sam Iseman. I would like to remember the late Sam Iseman for his dedication and inspiration.

This second Prentice Hall edition (fifth historical edition) continues to innovate. We are very happy to welcome Dr. Jeff Beck and his computer exercise and tutorial to the *Workbook*. Dr. Beck has worked for several years with Marriott Hotels and is currently holds the Charles Lanphere professorship in Hotel Administration at Oklahoma State University. In that capacity he manages the link between the operations of The Hotel at OSU, which the School of Hotel and Restaurant operates as a teaching hotel, and the academic program's classes. He brings his experience in the use of the property management system to the design of the computer tutorial section of the *Workbook*.

Dr. Gail Sammons has rewritten Problem Sets I and II and has refreshed and updated the Sample Night Audit Exercise. She has also further redesigned the forms used in the problem sets. Gail also continued the responsibility of managing the compilation of the final text.

And last, with great excitement, we have added a new section on Front Office Operational Auditing. The Front Office Operational Audit, which can be used as both a teaching/learning tool and as a practical management tool in hotels, has resulted from over seven years of research.

I received comments and suggestions from other instructors who have used this book and incorporated them into this edition. Please continue to communicate them to any of us.

Patrick J. Moreo, Ed.D., CHA

Notes to Instructors

- Enough forms are included for two problem sets.

- We have found it quite beneficial to change one or two numbers for each class so that some of the final figures will be different from semester to semester. This is relatively simple to do, especially if you change those figures that will not affect the cash totals. If you contact the authors, we can provide you with further details on implementing this system with a minimum of effort.

  Also available is an Instructor's Guide that contains both hard copy solution sets and a diskette with these same solution sets stored electronically. The solution sets may also be used to generate differences in the problem sets themselves, helping to make certain that students each semester, and in each section, are challenged with problem sets that are uniquely their own.

- You may request the Instructor's Guide by contacting your local Prentice-Hall sales representative, or by contacting any of us authors directly, as per below:

Dr. Patrick J. Moreo
School of Hotel and Restaurant Administration
210 HESW
Oklahoma State University
Stillwater, OK 74074   Office phone: 405-744-8484
pmoreo@okstate.edu

Dr. Gail Sammons
William F. Harrah College of Hotel Administration
University of Nevada, Las Vegas
4505 Maryland Parkway Box 456021
Las Vegas, NV 89154-6021   Office phone: 702-895-4462
sammons@ccmail.nevada.edu

Dr. Jeff Beck
School of Hotel and Restaurant Administration
210 HESW
Oklahoma State University
Stillwater, OK 74074   Office phone: 405-744-8483
beckja@okstate.edu

Notes to Students

This workbook is designed to help you to understand the basics of designing and operating a system of guest accounts receivable and guest status management in the front office of a hotel or other lodging facility. It has been our experience and our belief after teaching hundreds of students and conducting discussions with alumni in the years after they have graduated that an understanding of the "manual" system is crucial to the comprehension of other systems.

Use of this manual system will make it very easy for you to see each component of the front office accounting and guest management system and how each component is interrelated to all of the other parts of the system, because you will actually be manipulating each of these parts yourself.

With this basic understanding, future application of the knowledge gained makes a lot more sense. So, when you begin to learn about the plethora of computer systems, you will know what these systems are supposed to do—because you have done it yourself!

Indeed, you will then to be able to clearly see what it is you would like the computer programs to do and what is no longer necessary compared to the manual or electronic systems. The perfect followup to performing these manual exercises is to do the same thing using a computer front office or property management system such as M.S.I., H.I.S., Lodgistix, Fidelio, or any of a number of fine software packages available either in your next job position, or in a school computer laboratory. Computer systems will continue to rapidly change over the years. The practice and understanding you will receive from these exercises provides excellent preparation for the development and change which we will continue to see.

In order to help with this understanding and transition, we have included a computerized section in this workbook. The disk and instructions will illustrate for you several things: First, what does the "environment" of a property management system look like? Reservations, registration, "room rack," folios, and guest tracking and communications are greatly automated and simplified. Second, what does computer design mean in operating the hotel? An entry generally needs to be made only one time. Mistakes are much less frequent because we are not manually copying information from one place to another. Posting can be done from the point of sale in the hotel. And finally, the same guest information is available to many critical places on the property simultaneously. So, the front office, housekeeping, sales and catering, reservations, telecommunications, service staff, room service, and restaurants can all have the same live access. Transactions are greatly speeded up and accuracy increased.

But probably one of the most important things that you should realize as you walk through the computerized example set is what it means for management. As guest service agents, supervisors, department heads, and managers, we are no longer bound by availability of equipment and information in one place. A service agent does not have to go to a particular file in the front office. Restaurants no longer have to wait on a phone to check to see if someone is registered and authorized to make a charge. Information is available simultaneously throughout the property. Thus, jobs themselves can be designed in very different ways. Each computer terminal provides everything we need to provide guest service, information, and accounting. Consider this as you are doing the computer exercise.

Please be sure to do the problems in the same order they would be done during the hotel work day. In the manual problems, don't try to do the transcript first, for example. Get the check-ins, the folios, and the voucher posting done first. If you do, you'll have a much better understanding of what's going on and the problems will be more fun and less time-consuming.

Manual Night Audit Instructions and Exercise

Section 1
The Night Audit of Accounts Receivable

The purposes of performing the night audit include the following:

1. Ensure that each guest account is correct.

2. Ensure that charges and credits have been properly posted for accounting purposes.

3. Provide succinct, valuable management reports summarizing the salient features of the day's business.

The methods used to accomplish these purposes are varied, but can be summarized into three major categories for simplicity's sake:

- **Manual method**—the hand transcript. Only a few of the smallest lodging properties continue to use the hand transcript in practice. But there are still some! Understanding the manual method is still the key to understanding any other system that has evolved, especially computer property management systems. The manual system forces you to proceed through the system and look at each entry separately. Much of what computer software does is based on what happened in previous manual systems.

- **Electronic methods**—includes the use of posting machines (e.g., Micros, NCR, etc.) Most of these systems generally required the maintenance of paper folios to be used with limited machine memory. They have been almost completely phased out, but remain important in understanding the historical development of computer property management systems.

- **Computer methods**—including both PC (personal computer)-driven systems and mainframe systems.

  1. PCs have customarily been considered small-scale computer systems quite often integrating all front office functions including reservations and room status as well as the accounting functions for guests' accounts receivable. Depending upon the size of the property and design of the system, the PC can operate as a stand-alone computer or be integrated on a Local Area Network (LAN).

  2. Full-scale mainframe computer systems generally consist of a hotel-wide system including many terminals and driven from one large central processing unit. The scope and use of these mainframe systems is rapidly changing as the individual PCs and LANs become extremely powerful.

In the past, the PC and the mainframe have been considered two very distinct types of computer systems. The last few years have seen tremendous advances in technology. These advances continue and now allow small properties to begin with systems of appropriate size and complexity for the property, but with the ability to expand both the size and computer sophistication of software and hardware with growth.

The concept of networking PCs together has made the possibility of computer use desirable in virtually any size or type property. Nevertheless, an understanding of the basic concepts as they are put forth in the manual system is crucial to making these evolving applications.

Finally, be prepared for many different applications in the field. While most hotel and lodging properties are at least partially computerized, there are still a few especially smaller ones that are not. The principles of accuracy of guest bills, proper distribution of charges among operating departments, and availability of succinct management reports remain the same. Executing them becomes more efficient, faster, and simpler as computer applications become more sophisticated.

In any case, the following formula summarizes the requirements for the night audit to be satisfactorily completed regardless of which system is used.

Section 2
Night Audit Formula

THE NIGHT AUDIT FORMULA

THE CALCULATION	*THE PROOF*
TODAY'S OPENING GUEST LEDGER BALANCE (from folios)	(Must equal yesterday's closing balance)
+TODAY'S CHARGES (from folios)	(Must equal today's voucher totals for each department, which must equal departmental control totals for each department)
−TODAY'S CREDITS (from folios)	(Must equal today's voucher totals for each department, or cash, or transfers as appropriate and must equal any departmental control total as appropriate
=TODAY'S CLOSING GUEST LEDGER BALANCE	(Must equal the total of the folio closing balances on folio balance sheet, tape, or total)

Immediately following the directions for student use on the next page, there is a sample job analysis for the manual night audit. It is included as a guideline to arrive at a management perspective concerning the night audit. It should serve as a reminder that similar outlines should be prepared for the night audit (or any front office job) regardless of what system is used to perform the audit. The analysis is a training aid and provides a measure of security for new employees, especially the first few shifts they work by themselves.

To be sure, the analysis included here is simply a sample. Most hotels have their own particular ways of doing things. Yet, the basic procedures are undoubtedly common to all lodging facilities. Certainly, management could take the analysis further, fleshing it out to a full-scale procedural manual by explaining each job analysis step in more detail and illustrating the steps with sample calculations, diagrams, forms, and photographs.

In front office systems using electronic posting machines or computers, clearly labeled diagrams and photographs should illustrate the function and position of each key, switch, or screen in the proper order. This is primarily for the benefit of the employee who is not familiar with the system and so should be as simply and clearly stated as possible.

Most contemporary computer software should include optional "help" instructions directly in the program sequence, thus making it as user friendly as possible. By making the help screens optional, they are available when needed but not necessary to the function of the program, and thus do not slow down the seasoned user. More powerful graphics and expanded memory also make it possible for screen displays to be very illustrative and self-explanatory. The more closely the screen can resemble the configuration of the hotel or the guest bill itself, for example, the simpler it will be for associates to train on and use.

Finally, the analysis for the manual night audit should serve as an aid to the student who is going to complete one or more of the problem sets contained herein in conjunction with classroom lectures and any accompanying textbook and the completed sample night audit forms that follow the analysis.

Section 3
Directions for the Student Exercise

The *Front Office Operations and Auditing Workbook* actually encapsulates the entire hotel day's work in the front office, including check-ins, check-outs, postings, and other transactions. You actually perform an entire day's front office transactions before beginning the audit itself. The preliminary front office guest management part of the exercise should put front office accounting operations into cycled perspective. For this reason, we strongly urge you to complete each problem in the order in which the components of that problem appear—as though you were working in the front office from the morning on through the day and evening shifts and finally ending with the night audit itself.

So, in order for you to realize the full benefit of the exercise, it is best to approach it as realistically as possible. This means that the transactions should be made in roughly the same order in which they would chronologically happen. Thus all of the check-ins, check-outs, postings, and other transactions should be completed prior to beginning the night audit procedure itself. You should refer to whichever main text or handouts you are using for the course as a guide for guest registration, folio preparation, and so on.

In other words, you will, for the first part of the exercise, do the work of the day and swing shift receptionist and cashiers. You will then begin the work of the night auditor. At that point it would be beneficial to begin to use the sample "Job Analysis" as an instructional guide.

Section 4
Sample Job Analysis for Manual Night Audit

1. Read log book and any new memos or communications.

2. Obtain any necessary information from the off-going shift.

3. Count cash (if using common bank with other shifts).

4. Post any charges that still remain from the previous shift.

5. Prepare the Room and House Count Report (if not done by a night clerk).

6. Total charge and credit vouchers by department fastening an adding machine tape to each packet of vouchers.

7. Check voucher packet totals against departmental control sheet totals if available.

8.   a.   Post room and tax to each folio.

        b.   Add total charges, total credits, and closing balance for each folio.

        c.   Post the charges and credits from each folio to the transcript sheet.

9. When all folios are posted to the transcript, add the total charges, the total credits and the closing balance for each room entered on the transcript.

10. Foot and cross-foot the transcript (add rows across and columns down). This simply insures that there are no mathematical errors; it does not mean the audit is in balance.

11. Verify that the departmental total columns on the transcript agree with the voucher totals (and with the departmental control sheet totals) for each department.

12. Make an adding machine tape that includes the closing balance of each guest ledger folio. The total of the tape is the guest ledger closing balance for today.

13. Verify that the total guest ledger balance for today according to the adding machine tape of the folio closing balances agrees with the total net guest ledger closing balance as shown on the transcript. The night audit is in balance if the totals indicated to this point agree.

14. Carry forward the closing balance for each room on today's transcript as the opening balance on tomorrow's transcript.

Section 5
Sample Night Audit Exercise for the University Inn

- This exercise is an example of performing the night audit.

- Included at the end of the exercise are the completed cash sheet, cash envelope, room and house count sheet, and the transcript sheet.

- Brief notes appear on these completed forms to help you understand how the documents tie together. Of course, you shouldn't write these notes on your forms when you do the subsequent problems.

****

Sample Exercise

Following are the guest ledger balances at the close of the night audit for April 24. They become the opening balances for April 25.

Room #	Guest Names	# of Guests	Room Rate	Opening Balance for April 25, 20__
202	Mr. Rocky Roach	1	$50.00	$63.48
207	Mr. and Mrs. Phil Up	2	$50.00	$12.25
208	Mr. Drew Down	1	$75.00	$156.04
210	Mr. Stan Ipslinski	1	$50.00	$74.00

The following are the summaries of the departmental control sheets and other transactions for April 25.

1. Mr. Roach pays his account with cash and checks out after his charge is posted.

2. Mr. Down in 208 pays $150.00 on account and will stay another night. His room rents for $75.00.

8

3. Mr. and Mrs. Francisco Ramos and child of 20 Forbes Park, Manila, Philippines check into room 201 at $100.00 per night. They will stay three nights.

4. Mr. Leonardo Da Vinci checks into room 204. He had an advance deposit in the City Ledger of $75.00. He will stay two nights and is from 500 Broadway, New York, NY 10001. His rate is $75.00.

5. Mr. and Mrs. Ramos in room 201 have a tip paid-out to the restaurant for $2.50.

6. Ms. Sadie Silver and Ms. Nelly Nod check into room 206. The total room rate is $84.00. They are with the Kold Kreem Company of 1 Main Street, Union City, NJ 10033. They will stay one night.

7. Rabbi Jacob Josephson checks into room 209 for one week at the daily rate of $48.00. He is from 25 Park Place, New York, NY 10002.

8. Mr. Ipslinski in room 210 complains to the Assistant Manager that his shirt was not folded as he had requested, but was placed on a hanger instead. The Assistant Manager authorizes an allowance of $5.00 off his laundry charge from April 24.

9. Mr. Ipslinski, in room 210, pays his account with an American Express credit card and checks out as there are no further charges.

10. Mr. and Mrs. Conrad Vanderbuilt check into room 210 for one week at the daily rate of $90.00 per day. They have a $90.00 advance deposit in the City Ledger and reside at 201 Magnolia Lane, Oil City, TX 92543.

11. A C.O.D. package arrives for Mr. Vanderbuilt (room 210) for which the cashier makes a $5.72 paid-out to the postman.

12. Mr. and Mrs. Up (room 207) have requested that $16.40 of Mr. Down's bill be transferred to their account.

13. Mr. and Mrs. Up (room 207) pay with travelers' checks after their charge is posted and check out.

14. Mr. and Mrs. Salvatore Fertilla and their five children check into rooms 202/203. The total rate is $150.00. They will stay for one night and are from 27 Lombard Street, San Francisco, CA 88552.

15. Flowers from the Daisy Flower Shop arrive for Mr. Vanderbuilt (room 210) for which the cashier makes a paid-out of $30.50.

16. Mr. and Mrs. Fertilla (rooms 202/203) pay $175.00 on account by personal check.

17. Ms. Silver (room 206) pays $6.27 on account.

18. Mr. and Mrs. Pat Moreo and child, of the University of Nevada, Las Vegas, check into room 207. The room is an $40.00 special rate. They pay for two nights room and tax at check-in with an approved personal check.

Restaurant Summary April 25, 20__			Beverage Summary April 25, 20__		
201	(Ramos)	$15.00	201	(Ramos)	$7.50
202	(Roach)	$5.75	204	(Da Vinci)	$10.50
202/3	(Fertilla)	$27.00	208	(Down)	$9.50
202/3	(Fertilla)	$58.00	206	(Nod)	$6.50
206	(Silver)	$8.19	210	(Vanderbuilt)	$52.75
210	(Vanderbuilt)	$120.00			
206	(Nod)	$9.01			
209	(Josephson)	$8.75			

Local Telephone Summary April 25, 20__			Long Distance Telephone Summary April 25, 20__		
204	(Da Vinci)	$2.00	202/3	(Fertilla)	$3.81
202/3	(Fertilla)	$3.00	206	(Silver)	$6.27
209	(Josephson)	$2.00	210	(Vanderbuilt)	$57.50
209	(Josephson)	$2.00	208	(Down)	$2.80
210	(Vanderbuilt)	$1.00	207	(Up)	$8.16
207	(Moreo)	$2.00	207	(Moreo)	$3.25

Notes:

1. Room tax is computed at 10%.

2. Blank folios have been provided for the rooms that were occupied on April 24. You need not be concerned with addresses for these guests if none are given. Assume that they already have registration cards on file.

3. The following are the contents of the cash drawer at the close of business. The drawer started with a $500.00 bank.

Personal Checks:		$175.00
		69.23
		88.00
Traveler's Checks:		210.00
Bills:	$20.00	110.00
	$10.00	90.00
	$5.00	150.00
	$1.00	38.00
Coins:	.25	36.00
	.10	13.70
	.05	6.10
	.01	.56

Sample Night Audit Forms for the University Inn for this sample audit are shown in this order on the following pages.

1. Sample Registration Cards

2. Sample Folio

3. Sample Folio Bucket Balance Sheet

4. Sample Control Sheets

5. Sample Charge and Credit Vouchers

6. Sample Cash Envelope and Closing Bank

7. Sample Cash Sheet

8. Sample Room and House Count Sheet

9. Sample Daily Transcript

Sample Registration Cards

Folio #: _____

UNIVERSITY INN
Sample Registration Card

Date April 25, 20___

Name **Francisco Ramos**

Street **20 Forbes Park**

City **Manilla**   State **Philippines**   Zip Code _____

Affiliation _____

Arrival Date	Room #	Rate	Clerk	Departure Date	Credit Card #
April 25, 20__	201	$100	GS	April 28, 20___	

Remarks: 2 adults, 1 child _____

_____

_____

Money, jewels, and other valuable packages, must be placed in the safe in the office, otherwise the Management will not be responsible for any loss.

Cut along double lines   Cut along double lines

Folio #: _____

UNIVERSITY INN
Sample Registration Card

Date April 25, 20___

Name **Leonardo Da Vinci**

Street **500 Broadway**

City **NYC**   State **NY**   Zip Code **10001**

Affiliation _____

Arrival Date	Room #	Rate	Clerk	Departure Date	Credit Card #
April 25, 20__	204	$75	GS	April 27, 20__	

Remarks: Advance Deposit $75.00 _____

_____

_____

Money, jewels, and other valuable packages, must be placed in the safe in the office, otherwise the Management will not be responsible for any loss.

Folio #: _____

UNIVERSITY INN
Sample Folio

Guest's Name: **Francisco Ramos** _____   Room #: **201** _____

Departure Date: **April 28, 20__** _____   Today's Date: **April 25, 20__**

ALL ACCOUNTS ARE DUE WHEN RENDERED

DATE	April 25	April 26					
FORWARD	**$0.00**	**$135.00**					
Room	100.00						
Tax	10.00						
Restaurant	15.00						
Beverages	7.50						
Telephone - Local							
Telephone - L.D.							
Laundry							
Valet							
Misc. Charges							
Cash Disbursements	2.50						
Transfer Debits							
TOTAL DEBITS	**$135.00**						
Cash Received							
Allowances							
Transfer to City Ledger							
Transfer Credit							
TOTAL CREDITS	**$0.00**						
BALANCE FORWARD	**$135.00**						

UNIVERSITY INN
Sample Folio Bucket Balance Sheet

Date: **April 25, 20__**

This form takes the place of the calculator tape that would be run on folio balances. The final total of this tape should be equal to the total in column 22 on the daily transcript of the general ledger.

Room Number		Folio Closing Balance
201		$135.00
202		$81.81
203		$0.00
204		$20.00
205		$0.00
206		$116.10
207		($38.75)
208		$84.44
209		$65.55
210		$276.47
Total		**$740.62**

Sample Control Sheets

RESTAURANT DEPARTMENT CONTROL SHEET

NAME: Sample Audit   **DATE:** April 25, 20____

VOUCHER #	ROOM NO.	GUEST NAME	AMOUNT	MEMO
	201	Ramos	$15.00	
	202	Roach	$5.75	
	202/203	Fertilla	$27.00	
	202/203	Fertilla	$58.00	
	206	Silver	$8.19	
	210	Vanderbuilt	$120.00	
	206	Nod	$9.01	
	209	Josephson	$8.75	
Compares to Column #8 on				
Daily Transcript Sheet		**Total Amount**	$251.70	

BEVERAGE DEPARTMENT CONTROL SHEET

NAME: Sample Audit   **DATE:** April 25, 20____

VOUCHER #	ROOM NO.	GUEST NAME	AMOUNT	MEMO
	201	Ramos	$7.50	
	204	Da Vinci	$10.50	
	208	Down	$9.50	
	206	Nod	$6.50	
	210	Vanderbuilt	$52.75	
Compares to Column #8 on				
Daily Transcript Sheet		**Total Amount**	$86.75	

Sample Charge and Credit Vouchers

No. 1001 Sample Audit

UNIVERSITY INN

Restaurant — **Charge**
Department

Date: April 25, 20___ Room or Acct. No. **209**

Name: Rabbi Jacob Josephson

Date	Symbol	Amount

Do not write in above space

EXPLANATION: Dinner $8.75

Signed by: *GS*

Cut along double lines.

No. 1002 Sample Audit

UNIVERSITY INN

Cash Disbursement (Tip) — **Charge**
Department

Date: April 25, 20___ Room or Acct. No. **201**

Name: Francisco Ramos

Date	Symbol	Amount

Do not write in above space

EXPLANATION: Paid out tip to K.T. in restaurant $2.50

Signed by: *GS*

Cut along double lines.

No. 1003 Sample Audit

UNIVERSITY INN

Transfer — **Credit**
Department

Date: April 25, 20___ Room or Acct. No. **208**

Name: Mr. & Mrs. Phil Up

Date	Symbol	Amount

Do not write in above space

EXPLANATION: Transfer $6.40 from Mr. Down's (Room 208)   ($16.40)

Signed by: *GS*

No. 1004 Sample Audit

UNIVERSITY INN

Transfer — **Credit**
Department

Date: April 25, 20___ Room or Acct. No. **204**

Name: Leonardo Da Vinci

Date	Symbol	Amount

Do not write in above space

EXPLANATION: Transfer advance deposit from city ledger   ($75.00)

Signed by: *GS*

Sample Cash Envelope and Closing Bank

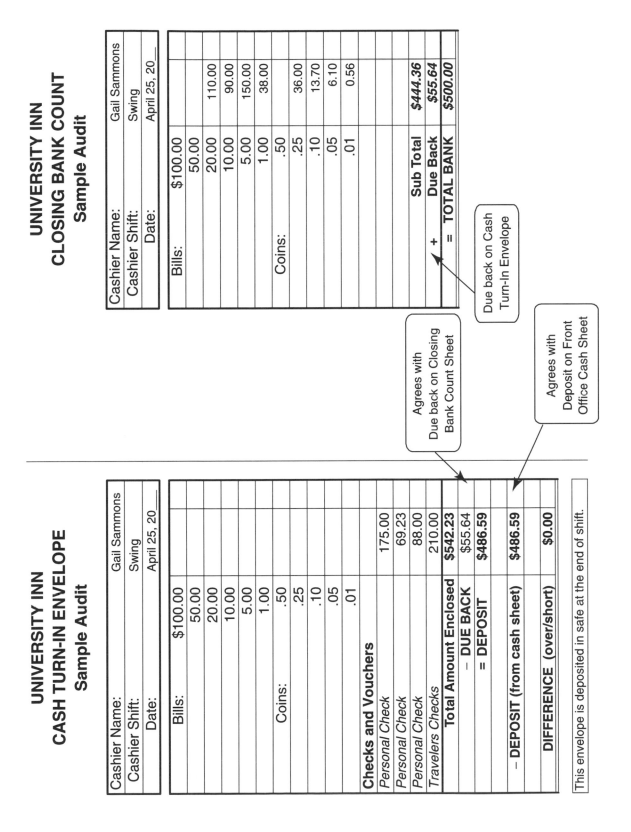

UNIVERSITY INN
CASH TURN-IN ENVELOPE
Sample Audit

Cashier Name:	Gail Sammons	
Cashier Shift:	Swing	
Date:	April 25, 20___	
Bills:	$100.00	
	50.00	
	20.00	
	10.00	
	5.00	
	1.00	
Coins:	.50	
	.25	
	.10	
	.05	
	.01	
Checks and Vouchers		
Personal Check		175.00
Personal Check		69.23
Personal Check		88.00
Travelers Checks		210.00
Total Amount Enclosed		$542.23
− DUE BACK		$55.64
= DEPOSIT		$486.59
− DEPOSIT (from cash sheet)		$486.59
DIFFERENCE (over/short)		$0.00

This envelope is deposited in safe at the end of shift.

UNIVERSITY INN
CLOSING BANK COUNT
Sample Audit

Cashier Name:	Gail Sammons	
Cashier Shift:	Swing	
Date:	April 25, 20___	
Bills:	$100.00	
	50.00	
	20.00	110.00
	10.00	90.00
	5.00	150.00
	1.00	38.00
Coins:	.50	
	.25	36.00
	.10	13.70
	.05	6.10
	.01	0.56
	Sub Total	$444.36
+	Due Back	$55.64
=	TOTAL BANK	$500.00

Due back on Cash Turn-In Envelope

Agrees with Due back on Closing Bank Count Sheet

Agrees with Deposit on Front Office Cash Sheet

23

Sample Room and House Count Sheet

UNIVERSITY INN
ROOM AND HOUSE COUNT SHEET
Sample Audit

Date: April 25, 20____

Room Reconciliation

	No. of Rooms	No. of Persons	Room Value	Tax Value
Yesterday	4	5	$150.00	$15.00
+ Arrivals	8	19	587	58.7
= Total	12	24	737	73.7
– Departures	3	4	75	7.5
= **Today**	9	20	$662.00	$66.20

Agrees with totals for columns 3, 5, and 6 respectively on transcript

Room Statistics

Rooms Available	10
Rooms Occupied	9
House Count	20
Average Rate per Occupied Room	$73.56
Average Rate per Guest	$33.10
Percentage of Occupancy	
Average Number of Guests per Room	2.2

Usually prepared from room rack.

Room #	No. of Guests	Tax	Room Rate
201	3	$10.00	$100.00
202/3	7	15.00	150.00
203	See Room 202		
204	1	7.50	75.00
205			
206	2	8.40	84.00
207	3	4.00	40.00
208	1	7.50	75.00
209	1	4.80	48.00
210	2	9.00	90.00
TOTAL	$20.00	$66.20	$662.00

Agrees with totals for columns 3, 5, and 6 respectively on transcript

27

Section 6
Night Audit Exercise for the University Inn
Problem Set I

- This exercise consists of performing the night audit using the hand transcript for the 10-room University Inn for November 13, 20___ .

- Please read this <u>entire</u> exercise <u>before</u> you begin completing any of the forms.

****

Exercise

Following are the guest ledger balances at the close of the night audit for November 12. They become the opening balances for November 13.

Room #	Guest Names	# of Guests	Room Rate	Opening Balance For November 13, 20__
202	Mr. Rocky Roach	1	$75.00	$87.18
207	Mr. and Mrs. Phil Up	2	$100.00	$112.25
208	Mr. Drew Down	1	$75.00	$86.04
210	Mr. Stan Ipslinski	1	$75.00	$264.00

Following are summaries of the departmental control sheets and other transactions for November 13:

1. Mr. Roach in room 202 pays his account in cash and checks out after his charge is posted.

2. Mr. Down in room 208 pays $85.00 cash on account and will stay another night.

3. Mr. and Mrs. Francisco Ramos and child of 20 Forbes Park, Manila, Philippines check into room 201 at $100.00 per night. They will stay three nights.

4. Mr. Leonardo Da Vinci checks into room 204. He had an advance deposit in the City Ledger of $75.00. He will stay two nights and is from 500 Broadway, New York, NY 10001. His rate is $75.00.

5. Ms. Sadie Silver and Ms. Nelly Nod check into room 206. The total room rate is $84.00. They are with the Kold Kreem Company of 1 Main Street, Union City, NJ 10011. They will stay one night.

6. Mr. and Mrs. Ramos (room 201) have a tip paid-out to the restaurant for $2.50.

7. Rabbi Jacob Josephson checks into room 209 for one week at the daily rate of $48.00. He is from 25 Park Place, New York, NY 10002.

8. Mr. Ipslinski in room 210 complains to the Assistant Manager that his shirt was not folded as he had requested, but was placed on a hangar instead. The Assistant Manager authorizes an allowance of $6.00 off his laundry charge from November 12.

9. Mr. Ipslinski (room 210) pays his account with a Visa credit card, and checks out.

10. Mr. and Mrs. Conrad Vanderbuilt check into room 210 for one week at the daily rate of $90.00 per day. They have an $90.00 advance deposit in the City Ledger and reside at 201 Magnolia Lane, Oil City, TX 92543.

11. A C.O.D. package arrives for Mr. Vanderbuilt (room 210) for which the cashier makes a $16.72 paid-out to the postman.

12. Mr. and Mrs. Up in room 207 have requested that $16.00 of Mr. Down's (room 208) bill be transferred to their account.

13. Mr. and Mrs. Up (room 207) pay with traveler's checks after their charge is posted and check out.

14. Mr. and Mrs. Salvatore Fertilla and their five children check into rooms 202/203. The total rate is $150.00. They will stay for one night and are from 27 Lombard Street, San Francisco, CA 88552.

15. Flowers from the Daisy Flower Shop arrive for Mr. Vanderbuilt (room 210) for which the cashier makes a paid-out of $40.50.

16. Mr. and Mrs. Fertilla (room 202) pay $175.00 by personal check on account.

17. Ms. Silver (room 206) pays $9.27 on account.

18. Mr. and Mrs. Pat Moreo and child, of the University of Nevada, Las Vegas, check into room 207. The room is an $40.00 special rate. They pay for two nights room and tax in advance with an approved personal check.

Restaurant Summary November 13, 20__				Beverage Summary November 13, 20__		
201	(Ramos)	$10.00		201	(Ramos)	$13.50
202	(Roach)	$6.75		204	(Da Vinci)	$8.00
202/3	(Fertilla)	$18.00		208	(Down)	$16.00
202/3	(Fertilla)	$38.00		206	(Nod)	$5.50
206	(Silver)	$9.95		210	(Vanderbuilt)	$34.25
206	(Nod)	$10.00				
210	(Vanderbuilt)	$120.00				
209	(Josephson)	$18.75				

Local Telephone Summary November 13, 20__				Long Distance Telephone Summary November 13, 20__		
204	(Da Vinci)	$2.00		202/3	(Fertilla)	$3.81
202/3	(Fertilla)	$6.00		206	(Silver)	$9.27
209	(Josephson)	$4.00		210	(Vanderbuilt)	$7.50
209	(Josephson)	$6.00		208	(Down)	$5.80
210	(Vanderbuilt)	$1.00		207	(Up)	$8.16
207	(Moreo)	$1.00		207	(Moreo)	$6.25

Notes:

1. Room tax is computed at 10%.

2. Blank folios have been provided for the rooms that were occupied on November 12. You need not be concerned with addresses for these guests if none are given. Assume that they already have registration cards on file.

3. The following are the contents of the cash drawer at the close of business. The drawer started with a $500.00 bank.

Personal Checks:		$263.00
Traveler's Checks:		360.00
Bills:	$20.00	120.00
	$10.00	90.00
	$5.00	110.00
	$1.00	84.00
Coins:	.25	23.00
	.10	13.70
	.05	4.80
	.01	.46

Section 7
Night Audit Exercise for the University Inn
Problem Set II

- This exercise consists of performing the night audit using the hand transcript for the ten-room University Inn for February 4, 20___.

- Please read this <u>entire</u> exercise <u>before</u> you begin completing any of the forms.

****

Exercise

Following are the guest ledger balances at the close of the night audit for February 3. They become the opening balances for February 4.

Room #	Guest Names	# of Guests	Room Rate	Opening Balance For February 4, 20__
201	Mr. and Mrs. F. Ramos	2	$150.00	$159.00
202/203	Mr. and Mrs. S. Fertilla	7	$150.00	($57.79)
204	Mr. L. Da Vinci	1	$75.00	$28.00
206	Ms. S. Silver	1	$42.00	$61.25
206	Ms. N. Nod	1	$42.00	$72.00
207	Mr. and Mrs. P. Moreo	3	$40.00	($25.75)
208	Mr. D. Down	1	$75.00	$81.90
209	Rabbi J. Josephson	1	$48.00	$40.00
210	Mr. and Mrs. C. Vanderbuilt	2	$150.00	$325.00

Following are the transactions and summaries of the departmental charges for February 4.

1. Dr. and Mrs. John Rhodes check into Room 205 for four nights. Their address is UC Davis, CA 89623. The room rate is $120 per night. They had an advance deposit of $132.00. In addition, they pay another $250 on account with a personal check.

34

2. Mr. Down checks out of room 208. He pays his account with travelers' checks.

3. The Fertilla family checks out of 202/203 with no further charges. Their credit balance must be returned to them.

4. Mr. and Mrs. Moreo check out of room 207 (one night early). They ask that $18.75 that was charged to Josephson's account in room 209 be transferred to their account first. They have a tip paid-out for $5. They pay their balance in cash.

5. Ms. Elaine Martucci of the Marine Midland Trust Co., Rochester, NY 14000 checks into room 203. The rate is $84 per night. She will pay with Visa.

6. Ms. Nod and Ms. Silver check out of room 206. Nod pays her account with cash. Silver pays with Visa.

7. Dr. Rhodes (room 205) has a miscellaneous paid-out of $9.25 for a fax sent to U.C. Davis.

8. Mr. Ramos in Room 201 has a C.O.D. delivery of theater tickets arrive for which he has authorized a paid-out amount of $96.

9. Mr. Da Vinci checks out of room 204. He pays his account with a Diner's Club card.

10. Mr. Richard Sullivan of 1701 Mission Vista Drive, San Diego, CA 87524, checks into room 204. The rate is $75.00 per night. He will pay with an American Express.

11. Mr. Sullivan of room 204 has a tip paid-out of $5.50.

12. Mr. Vanderbuilt of room 210 has a tip paid-out for $8.00.

13. Dr. Marie and Mr. Anthony Lucca of Temple University, Philadelphia, PA 12201, check into room 208 at a nightly rate of $150. They had an advance reservation deposit of $125. They will pay the remainder of their account with Master Card.

14. Ms. Stephanie Baumweiss checks into room 202. Her address is Van Camps Publishing Co., McCormick Place, Chicago, IL 66220. She will stay one night at a $75 room rate. She will be a direct billing.

15. Mr. Oscar Lopez and Mr. George Whipple of the Washington Publishing Co., 718 Broadway, New York, NY 10001, check into room 207. They are unsure of how many nights they will stay. Mr. Lopez will pay with an American Express Card, and Mr. Whipple will pay with a Mastercard. The room rate is $100 per night.

16. Mr. Harvey Shade of 807 Main Street, Frisbee, OH 32221, checks into room 206 at a rate of $75 per night. He will stay two nights; he will pay in cash. He anticipates charges and so pays $200 on account with a personal check.

17. Mr. Lucca in room 208 has a $7 tip paid-out.

18. Mr. Vanderbuilt (room 210) asked to look at his account and tells us that he did not get through on one of the long distance calls for which he was billed yesterday. The assistant front office manager authorizes a Long Distance Telephone Adjustment of $7.50.

Restaurant Summary February 4, 20__			Beverage Summary February 4, 20__		
207	(Moreo)	$15.75	210	(Vanderbuilt)	$32.00
206	(Silver)	$4.50	201	(Ramos)	$4.25
201	(Ramos)	$18.75	207	(Lopez)	$7.00
204	(Da Vinci)	$6.50	203	(Martucci)	$27.75
204	(Sullivan)	$15.50	207	(Whipple)	$6.75
208	(Lucca)	$40.00			
210	(Vanderbuilt)	$178.00			
205	(Rhodes)	$68.00			

Local Telephone Summary February 4, 20__			Long Distance Telephone Summary February 4, 20__		
204	(Da Vinci)	$2.00	206	(Nod)	$6.78
204	(Sullivan)	$1.00	204	(Da Vinci)	$10.60
210	(Vanderbuilt)	$3.00	201	(Ramos)	$7.80
203	(Martucci)	$1.00	203	(Martucci)	$4.55
208	(Lucca)	$1.00			

Notes:

1. Room tax is computed at 10%.

2. The following are the contents of the cash drawer at the close of business. The drawer started with a $500.00 bank.

36

Personal Checks:		$250.00; 200.00
Travelers' Checks:		220.00
Bills:	$20.00	80.00
	$10.00	80.00
	$5.00	40.00
	$1.00	42.00
Coins:	.25	12.25
	.10	6.30
	.05	4.55
	.01	.79

Section 8
Instructions and Use for Front Office
Operations and Night Audit
Workbook Companion CD v1.3*

The companion CD was created to familiarize the student with front office operations using a property management system such as *WinPM* from Multi-Systems, Inc. This tutorial is designed to lead students through the primary operations that occur at the front desk. The results of a brief quiz, available at the end of the tutorial, can be printed out for hand in.

System Requirements

This tutorial is designed to run on Windows 3.1, 95, and 98.

The minimum hardware requirements for operation:

A Pentium processor-based PC

32 megabytes of RAM

Color monitor set to 640 x 480 screen size with a minimum of 256 color resolution

4x CD-ROM

A printer for the tutorial quiz.

A soundcard is helpful, but not required.

Operation

Startup

This CD is designed to automatically start once placed in the CD-ROM tray. Depending on the processor speed and amount of memory on the machine, the program will start immediately or take 10 to 20 seconds to load. The average loading time on a Pentium 200 machine is 15 seconds. If the tutorial does not automatically start, the user should navigate to the File list for the CD using the appropriate drive letter (typically D:) and double-click on **FOops1_3.exe** to begin.

*All WinPM screens copyright Multi-Systems, Inc.

Operating the Tutorial

The tutorial begins with a welcome screen that provides background information on the tutorial. By continuing, the user can get instructions on how to navigate in the tutorial. A log-in is required. The password requested will be required for each subsequent use of the tutorial. The password should be all letters, upper or lower case. The password will also be required to complete the tutorial quiz. **The user should write down the password somewhere secure, as it will be needed again.**

The Reservations, Front Office, and Tutorial quiz modules are separate. The user cannot navigate between these modules without exiting out of one section back to the main menu and navigating to another module. Each section contains a module that the user can expect to complete in approximately 15 minutes. At the beginning of each section ia an introduction with learning objectives for the section; at the end is a summary of what was covered. The user may wish to take notes as he or she proceeds through the section.

Taking the Quiz

The quiz consists of fifteen multiple-choice questions. At the beginning is a practice question with instructions and feedback on how to take the quiz. The quiz allows two guesses at each question, but if the question is answered correctly on the first try, the user is prompted to proceed to the next question. At the end, the user may print out the results and exit the tutorial, or exit the tutorial without printing out the results.

Further Information/Feedback

This tutorial was designed with the user in mind. Sometimes errors in design and programming do occur. Therefore, if you as the student or faculty user have any questions, please feel free to contact me.

In that same spirit, I welcome feedback on how to improve this tutorial!

Jeff Beck, Ph.D.
Charles Lanphere Professor of Hotel Administration
School of Hotel and Restaurant Administration
Oklahoma State University
210 HESW
Stillwater, OK 74078
beckja@okstate.edu

September 1, 2000

If a hotel chooses not to use front line employees to complete the audit, it becomes crucial to make certain that they understand why the hotel does the audit. Reviewing the results with the hourly associates is also important. The first time around, a property might want to employ an outsider (third-party agent) to plan and execute the audit. This person would bring the time necessary for this initial foray if time is a problem at the property. Nevertheless, these outside agents should involve all concerned.

Final Note for Students and Instructors

A complete copy of the *Front Office Operational Audit* can be found in Section 10. If your instructor has you use parts of the *Audit* as a guide for a property visit or an interview, remember that not all hotels will use all of the questions. In fact, the best way for you to use this is to read it in advance and then just have a few of the most important questions summarized into one or two main questions that you could ask to "get the ball rolling" in the interview. Trying to go through the questionnaire question by question in an interview would be very tedious for all involved!

On the other hand, you may find that you are in a position to coordinate a project in a hotel using either the entire questionnaire or parts of it. If that is the case, then be sure to involve the associates in its completion as suggested in the following instructions, which form the cover sheet of the *Audit* itself.

Finally, if you are visiting a property, be aware of how important it is to be professional in demeanor and appearance. Make an appointment well in advance. Confirm it again before leaving for the property. And, make certain to dress professionally. All of these will go a long way in showing how serious you are and how much you respect the hotel and the person you will be visiting. This, in turn, will gain you respect!

Section 10
Hotel Front Office Operational Audit Form*

AUDIT QUESTIONS	Yes ✔	No ✔	NA ✔	COMMENTS/ Followup Action
PERSONNEL				
General				
Is there an orientation program?				
Does the front office manager identify training needs for the department?				
Is there an employee training program in place?				
Are training manuals available for each employee function?				
Are personnel cross-trained when not in conflict with union regulations?				
Are performance appraisals conducted on a timely basis?				
Are all guest comments concerning employees shared with the individual employee involved as well as supervisory personnel?				
Personnel Audit				
Are required posters and logs on hand?				
Are job descriptions maintained and updated on a regular basis?				
Are employee disciplinary procedures and house rules in compliance with company policies and procedures?				
Do employee awards/incentives programs occur on a regular basis?				
Are summaries of employee turnover analyzed?				
Are drivers of property vehicles properly screened and licensed?				
Scheduling				
Are written staffing guidelines for proper scheduling developed and followed?				
Are staffing levels adjusted and evaluated as needed?				
Is use of overtime analyzed?				
Is overtime scheduled?				
Are scheduling decisions reviewed by management?				
Organization Development				
If organization goals and mission statements exist are they available to all employees?				
Are company policies communicated to departments and employees?				
Are staff meetings conducted on a timely basis?				
Are minutes of meetings communicated to employees when appropriate?				

*Copyright © 1997
Patrick J. Moreo, Ed.D., CHA Oklahoma State University
Gail Sammons, Ph.D., CHA University Of Nevada Las Vegas

AUDIT QUESTIONS	Yes ✔	No ✔	NA ✔	COMMENTS/ Followup Action
GUEST SERVICES				
General				
Does the front desk have proper signing so that guests don't wait in the wrong place?				
Are the procedures for guest waiting in lines for check-in/check-out frequently monitored and changed if necessary?				
Are procedures established for reception and processing of guests who are members of special hotel guest programs or who are destined for "special" (VIP, Club, Concierge, etc.) guest floors or sections?				
Are hotel guest service (restaurants, pool, etc.) hours known by front office staff?				
Are procedures established for processing guest mail?				
Are special procedures in place for processing guest express/special delivery mail?				
Are guest safety deposit box procedures established and implemented?				
Are affiliate (chain) current hotel directories available to the guests?				
Do front office receptionists and cashiers have friendly, positive attitudes?				
Telephone (PBX)				
Are phones answered promptly and courteously?				
Do telephone operators have full knowledge of hotel services as well as local services, attractions, and points of interest?				
Is an information directory maintained and accessible?				
Does the department provide for proper handling of messages taken: for guests in the hotel?				
guest with reservations?				
for meeting rooms?				
and rooms requesting no calls?				
In manual systems, are time stamps used on messages, phone charges, mail, and folios?				
In manual systems, are message lights turned off promptly?				
In automated systems, are unretrieved guest messages followed up periodically?				
Are procedures in place for wake-up calls?				
Are telephones for the hearing impaired available (in compliance with ADA audit): guest rooms?				
house phone?				
public phone?				
Do front office cashiers update local phone meters at check-out in semi-automatic systems?				
Are phone and operator service bills reviewed regularly for accuracy?				
Is credit received from telephone company for disputed calls?				
Are equipment rental charges checked periodically?				
Are local and long distance carriers reviewed regularly for quality, service, and pricing?				
In an automated system, is there a system for recording and reviewing phone charges for unoccupied or late checkout rooms?				

AUDIT QUESTIONS	Yes ✔	No ✔	NA ✔	COMMENTS/ Followup Action
GENERAL APPEARANCE				
General				
Is front entrance:				
kept clean and clear of trash?				
free of unnecessarily parked cars?				
fire lanes maintained at all times?				
Are lobby and public areas clean and in order and free of clutter?				
Is lighting inviting?				
Does the front desk have a clean appearance especially from the guest's perspective (e.g., free of disorderly and excessive credit card applications, signs, and brochures)?				
Are signs both necessary and appropriate to the setting?				
Is the hotel function board:				
appropriate to the setting, neat, and kept current?				
an assigned responsibility?				
Are concierge desk, bell stand, and other service areas attractive and neat in appearance (comfortable chairs, designer phone, fresh flowers, etc.)?				
Is storage of extra bell carts in a secured and out of sight area?				
Is the front desk set up for efficient operation?				
Staff				
Does someone monitor the appearance of staff periodically?				
Are all front office personnel:				
well groomed and neat?				
do they all have name tags and uniforms?				
do uniforms fit properly?				
Do front office staff present a professional image and appearance at all times?				
Bell Staff				
Do bell persons offer a standard guest greeting at door?				
Do door/bell staff screen guests in order to direct them to the appropriate check-in area if necessary?				
Are cars and cabs greeted promptly?				
Does the bell staff smile and converse with the guest in a friendly manner?				
Does the bell person/door attendant present a professional appearance and professional conduct at all times, even when guests are not directly present?				
Do bell persons provide an orientation while rooming guest that insures the guest is aware of all functions in the room as well as the services that the hotel has to offer?				
Does the bell staff thank the guest for his/her business?				
Can the bell staff give concise and accurate directions to local attractions and facilities?				
Are all service calls logged and timed, and is action time logged?				
Is the bell staff phone set up so that it can be answered at all times, even when someone is not present at bell desk?				
When a bell staff member is not available, is an alternate planned to provide service to the guest?				

AUDIT QUESTIONS	Yes ✔	No ✔	NA ✔	COMMENTS/ Followup Action
GENERAL APPEARANCE, continued				
Bell Staff, continued				
Are valet and laundry delivered promptly when received?				
Is orientation and information about the hotel provided by van drivers when transporting guests?				
Are written tour handling procedures provided to the bell staff?				
Are guests pressured to use bell staff if not desired?				
Are all bell staff aware of proper procedures in checking and holding luggage?				
Is guest checked luggage in a secure area with claim checks issued accordingly?				
Is luggage to be sent to the guest's room properly labeled?				
Are procedures documented to move luggage to guest room should guest wish to proceed to room without escort?				
Is the baggage storeroom clean and neat with luggage stacked neatly on the shelves?				
Is there a written procedure for handling claims of lost luggage?				
GUEST AND ROOM STATUS MANAGEMENT				
General				
Is the front office bulletin or status board kept up-to-date?				
Does the front office manager review correspondence on a daily basis?				
Are front office employees required: to read all relevant memos?				
to initial all relevant memos?				
Is a memo binder kept up-to-date?				
Is a log book used to monitor internal communication at the front desk?				
Is an end of shift checklist in use?				
Are there written procedures for front office employees in the event of equipment failure?				
Is there a control of inventories of paper supplies and other stock?				
If outside shoppers are used, are the results of past internal audits and reports reviewed in detail with all front office personnel?				
Are in-house files for folios and registration cards in good order with the ability to cross reference?				
Is a front office manual available to all front office, PBX employees, and bell staff?				
Is the front office manual updated to reflect all current policies and procedures?				
In the manual system, do telephone operators receive guest information promptly?				
Is guest history information collected and used by the front office and other departments?				
Does the front office staff use the guests' names?				

AUDIT QUESTIONS	Yes ✔	No ✔	NA ✔	COMMENTS/ Followup Action
GUEST AND ROOM STATUS MANAGEMENT, continued				
Rooms Management				
Are procedures used to ensure that maximum revenue is realized on additional earnings from items such as late check-outs, roll-aways, etc?				
Are procedures in place for maximizing multiple occupancy revenues?				
Are the names of all local front office and reservation managers in a current file?				
Are these individuals contacted regularly for overflow business and other formalities?				
Are there any recurring problems with daily room status controls and procedures? (*If so, note them in the comments column.*)				
Does the front office manager maintain control over out of order (off market) rooms to insure that they are returned for sale as soon as possible?				
Are room rates established in accordance with guidelines set by senior or corporate management?				
Are rack rates adhered to? (*If not, comment on major reasons why.*)				
Are room rate variances reported and explained daily?				
Are airline and other major discounts managed in any special way on nights approaching full occupancy?				
Is there an established procedure for discounting parlor or other nondedicated sleeping rooms when they are used for sleeping?				
Is there a policy for selling suites and other high-priced units?				
Are procedures in place for processing cancellations and no-shows?				
Are procedures in place to ensure billing of guaranteed no-shows?				
Are reasons indicated for "DID NOT STAY" guests who left the hotel without completing their stay?				
Are registration cards marked "DID NOT STAY" reviewed by management?				
Are VIP, handicap, and other special request rooms blocked early in the day?				
On nights approaching full occupancy, are reservations checked for duplicates periodically during the day?				
Is room availability assessed at regular intervals on nights the hotel is approaching full occupancy?				
On nights approaching full occupancy, are reservations assured by deposit or secured by guarantee blocked early enough in the day to ensure their availability?				
Is there a policy and procedure established for renting "special floor," handicapped, and other limited rooms at the front desk to prevent problems with a future block on those rooms?				
Guest Arrival				
Is there an adequate number of registration stations?				
Are special check-in procedures in place for processing group arrivals efficiently?				
Are front office employees knowledgeable concerning: acceptable credit cards?				
special promotion/packages/programs?				
special rates?				

AUDIT QUESTIONS	Yes ✔	No ✔	NA ✔	COMMENTS/ Followup Action
GUEST AND ROOM STATUS MANAGEMENT, continued				
Guest Arrival, continued				
special room types (e.g., nonsmoking, handicapped)?				
bed types in rooms?				
location of rooms?				
view from rooms?				
Are the explanations for codes, symbols, abbreviations, flags, etc. on both computer and manual parts of the front office readily available at each station?				
Are registration cards and folios complete including: guest signature?				
guest address?				
method of payment?				
ID, if necessary?				
time stamp, if necessary?				
At the time of check-in do clerks verbally verify the: correctness and spelling of the guest name and address?				
room type?				
date of departure?				
Does the front desk staff inquire if the guest would like a bell person?				
Are procedures in place that allow early arrivals to be roomed as quickly as possible and accommodated on their other needs?				
Does the front desk staff offer guest directions to the room if a bell person is not used?				
Are the following procedures evaluated for guests who must be walked?				
Priority on categories of guests who will be walked?				
Compensations for the inconvenience such as a complimentary night, discount, or gift?				
Apology letters from management for those guest who are walked?				
Are all walks recorded and analyzed?				
Are procedures and training established for handling "lost" reservations?				
Are guests preregistered as appropriate in both manual and computer system?				
Does the front office staff maintain eye contact with guests?				
Are rooms and rates assigned in a manner that mutually maximizes room revenue and guest satisfaction?				
Are express or other special check-out services explained?				
Does the front office staff inform guests of the services that the hotel offers, including revenue-generating areas such as restaurants and lounges?				
Does the front office staff adequately inform guests about features unique to the hotel such as the availability of continental breakfast, etc.?				
Does the front office staff double check to ensure that they are giving guests the correct room key?				
Is a welcome packet used for key presentation at check-in?				
Is there a policy for upgrading to be done on a selective basis as marketing needs dictate?				
Does reservations and/or the sales department notify the front office well in advance on group blocks and booking pace?				
Is group information clarified and checked with the sales department prior to the group's arrival?				

AUDIT QUESTIONS	Yes ✔	No ✔	NA ✔	COMMENTS/ Followup Action
GUEST AND ROOM STATUS MANAGEMENT, continued				
Guest Arrival, continued				
Is a VIP arrival report prepared and reviewed by the front office staff?				
Are all concerned departments such as housekeeping, telephone, bell staff, and food and beverage informed of VIP and handicapped arrivals?				
Are automated check-in systems evaluated/reviewed on a timely basis?				
Guest Departure				
Are expected check-outs flagged early in the day if the guest is scheduled to leave?				
Is there an adequate number of cashier stations?				
Is there an adequate number of automated check-out stations?				
Is there a drop box at the front desk for keys?				
Are all charges explained to the guest at the time of check-out?				
Is the guest thanked for his/her business?				
Are late check-outs processed properly?				
Are express check-out folios processed promptly?				
Are there special procedures in place to handle group check-outs or other large volume check-out situations?				
Are automated check-out systems evaluated/reviewed on a timely basis?				
Key Control / Security				
Is a par stock of keys established and kept at the front desk?				
Is the number of keys in stock at the front desk sufficient?				
Are key inventories taken on a regular basis?				
Are key requisition records kept and reviewed?				
Is storage of guest room keys secured?				
Do front office personnel refrain from giving out guest room numbers?				
Is key control reviewed on a regular basis?				
Are key issues recorded?				
Are keys requested from the guest at check-out?				
Does housekeeping return keys to the front desk on a daily basis?				
Are manufacturers' security recommendations followed for all locking systems?				
RESERVATIONS AND ROOM INVENTORY MANAGEMENT				
Reservation Procedures				
Is mail time stamped as it is received and processed?				
Are there adequate phone lines and staffing for incoming reservations?				
Is a room/rate availability board in the front office maintained and updated regularly?				
Is reservation correspondence filed by date and alphabetical order on a daily basis?				
Are rate cards, forms, and convention and house brochures available for guest correspondence?				
Are cancellation numbers provided for reservation cancellations?				
Is there a VIP list?				
Are there documented comp procedures for VIPs?				
Are VIPs and special requests blocked at time of reservation?				

AUDIT QUESTIONS	Yes ✔	No ✔	NA ✔	COMMENTS/ Followup Action
RESERVATIONS AND ROOM INVENTORY MANAGEMENT, continued				
Reservation Procedures, continued				
Are same day cancellations communicated between reservations and the front desk?				
Is there after-hours reservation coverage?				
If two reservation systems are used, are they compared for accuracy (e.g., internal reservations system and central reservations system)?				
Are confirmations sent on a timely basis and with a quality appearance?				
Are undeliverable confirmations so noted on the reservation for address accuracy?				
Are wait lists reviewed prior to opening up selling?				
For a manual reservation system: Is each reservation request recorded in a record of advance reservations, sometimes known as a tally book?				
Are cancellations or revisions subtracted and/or added to insure that the tally book is always accurate?				
If reservation cards are used, are they filed by date of arrival and alphabetically?				
Do reservationists explain the types of reservations to potential guests: guarantees?				
advance deposit?				
unsecured?				
Travel Agents				
Are travel agent commissions paid promptly?				
Do you analyze travel agency commission expenses (monthly)?				
Do you review business generated by travel agents?				
Rooms Inventory Control				
Is there a record of call conversion statistics?				
Do you set and review status controls and selling restrictions for rooms selling: minimum stays?				
closeout rate categories?				
Are rooms being sold in the most profitable order?				
Forecasting/Demand Analysis				
Do you research and analyze trends in the lodging industry?				
Do you conduct a local demand analysis of transient business?				
Do you compare demand to past years, months, weeks?				
Do you survey competition's rate structures on a regular basis?				
Do you accurately categorize and report occupancy, revenue, and average rate of each market segment, each night?				
Do you tabulate on a daily basis: no-show statistics?				
walk-in factors?				
early check-outs?				
Do you track accuracy of forecasts on a weekly/monthly basis, analyze discrepancies, and discuss strategies to improve?				

AUDIT QUESTIONS	Yes ✔	No ✔	NA ✔	COMMENTS/ Followup Action
RESERVATIONS AND ROOM INVENTORY MANAGEMENT, continued				
Forecasting/Demand Analysis, continued				
Does the reservations department contribute forecast information to: the annual budget?				
short-term forecasts?				
Are short-term forecasts prepared and distributed to operating departments: 10-day?				
3-day?				
Are there long-range forecasts?				
Group Rooms Control				
Is there a review of group rooming list due dates?				
Is there a review of incoming group pick-up?				
Is there a review of group tentative room blocks beyond option dates?				
GUEST LEDGER				
Credit				
Is a credit (limit) report maintained for each shift or each day?				
Are policies for guests who pay cash at check-in established and followed?				
Are policies for guests with advance deposits established and followed?				
Are check cashing and acceptance policies established and followed?				
Are direct billing procedures established and followed?				
Are clerks trained to be aware of potential skips and bad credit risks?				
Does a shift "bucket check" include a review of all imprinted credit card vouchers and authorization numbers?				
Are cashiers checking for late charges (breakfast, phone) at check-out?				
Guest Folios				
Are all corrections controlled and balanced?				
Are procedures established for the use of adjustments, allowances, discounts, and rebates?				
Does a company policy exist regarding adjustments to room revenue?				
Do the allowances indicate any specific problems with "sleepers," etc?				
Is there a procedure for notifying management of total charges over a set limit to any one guest's folio?				
Are guest folio balances that are very small reported in the morning to the manager?				
Are tax-exempt rooms properly accounted for and listed on the tax exemption report?				
Are outside vendor charges to the guest ledger (such as valet) properly reconciled?				
Is there a procedure for allocation of package plans?				
Is a bucket to computer check done in computerized operations, if necessary?				

AUDIT QUESTIONS	Yes ✔	No ✔	NA ✔	COMMENTS/ Followup Action
GUEST LEDGER				
Foreign Money Exchange				
Are rates of exchange for foreign currencies updated on a daily basis?				
Are rates of exchange for foreign currencies provided to a guest exchanging moneys?				
Are the policies and procedures regarding exchange of foreign currencies evaluated on a regular basis to ensure service to the guest while maintaining cash security?				
Manual Operation only:				
Are continuation folios marked to and from for proper cross-referencing?				
Are all folios balanced?				
time stamped?				
current?				
and properly classified as guest ledger?				
Is a bucket check done nightly?				
Is bucket audited daily and master accounts transferred to city ledger on a timely basis?				
Are alphabetical (registration cards) and numerical (folios by folio number) filing for departed guests done on a timely basis?				
Is security over all cash registers or cash drawers adequate?				
Are procedures for shift closing established and followed?				
Is there a review of cashiers reports?				
Do employees make cash drops on a timely basis, securing excess cash?				
Are deposit procedures in place and followed, including: witnessing and/or signing of sealed envelope?				
the transport of shift deposits to the drop safe?				
drop facilities constructed securely?				
Are there procedures for cash paid-outs (i.e., petty cash)?				
Do all paid-outs have proper documentation?				
Are cashier corrections, voids, and rebates documented and supported?				
Are all cash drawers kept locked and is access controlled so that accountability is maintained? *(i.e., Is there only one person per cash drawer?)*				
If banks are transferred or used by more than one shift, are the banks counted before and after every shift?				
Are duplicate house bank keys and the combination to the general cashier safe properly secured?				
Is there a schedule or inventory of all house banks?				
Is the house bank balance reconciled to the general ledger?				
Are cash drawers and banks audited on a regular basis?				
Are records kept of the cash drawer and bank audits?				
CITY LEDGER				
General				
Are procedures established for direct bill authorization?				
Is there a (manual or computer) direct bill authorization file of updated letters of authorization, with billing parameters defined?				

AUDIT QUESTIONS	Yes ✔	No ✔	NA ✔	COMMENTS/ Followup Action
CITY LEDGER, continued				
General, continued				
Are only authorized individuals permitted to sign direct billing accounts?				
Are past due accounts reviewed periodically to determine adequacy documentation of collection efforts?				
Are city ledger accounts receivable analyzed to determine: direct bills?				
sleepers?				
after departure (late) charges?				
prepaid accounts with charges?				
disputed accounts?				
delinquent accounts (over 60 days)?				
skips?				
tour vouchers?				
employee and intercompany accounts?				
and pay on departure accounts?				
Are procedures in place to properly age and act upon various city ledger categories?				
Is billing timely and in accordance with the established policy?				
Are turnaround times monitored for credit card receivable payments?				
Are procedures established and implemented for determining write-offs (e.g., sleepers or skippers)?				
Are accounting procedures implemented for trade outs, due bills, etc., and is the front office aware of them?				
Are procedures established for processing reservation no-shows guaranteed on credit cards through city ledger billing?				
Are written efficient master account handling procedures in place and implemented?				
Are returned checks analyzed for propriety, aging, and immediately redeposited?				
Is a procedure established for the disposition of money received on accounts previously written off?				
Are credit card charge backs reviewed on a timely basis?				
Advance Deposits				
Are procedures established for receiving, recording, and transferring of city ledger advance deposit payments if they are handled through the city ledger?				
Do group advance deposits shown in sales files and function book agree with posted folios?				
Are advance deposits recorded and logged by the reservations department by guest name and date of arrival?				
If manual folios are used, are the folios secured?				
Are advance deposit folios reconciled to either the general ledger or city ledger?				
Upon guest check-in, are advance deposits properly transferred?				
Are revenues or refunds processed promptly on unused deposits?				

AUDIT QUESTIONS	Yes ✔	No ✔	NA ✔	COMMENTS/ Followup Action
CREDIT CARD USAGE				
Are floor limits for each type of credit card set and reviewed periodically?				
Do cashiers know the floor limits for credit cards?				
Are policies in writing for expired or unauthorized credit cards; do employees have knowledge of, and follow these policies?				
Is an explanation of credit card procedures offered to a guest during check-in?				
Are all credit cards authorized?				
Are all credit card vouchers complete with an authorization number, account number, clerk's initials, and folio numbers?				
Are credit card imprinters dated correctly?				
Are credit cards imprinted on both registration cards and vouchers?				
NIGHT AUDIT				
General				
Are all night audit procedures clearly documented and readily available to night audit personnel?				
Is a night clerk summary: Comp list — Out of Order (off market) report completed?				
Are all exceptions explained: room rates, local telephone?				
Are room rates verified on all folios?				
Is room tax charged correctly?				
Are all tax exempt sales reported on the daily report with proper documentation support?				
Are long distance surcharges applied correctly?				
Are long distance calls taxed properly?				
Are bank cashier deposits checked against the daily report?				
Are all operating departments balanced?				
Is the night audit consistently in balance?				
Are daily night audit materials maintained in a consistent order and filed properly?				
Are copies of all vouchers kept on the property in a consistently organized system and with night audit documents?				
When the daily report and other required reports are generated, are at least all the following statistics included: rooms available and occupied?				
total guests?				
average daily room rate?				
average length of stay?				
percentage of double occupancy?				
percentage of occupancy?				
average rate per guest?				
room rate variances?				
Does the night auditor close the day and begin to operate on next day's business?				
Semi-automated and Manual Systems				
Are all room, tax, phone, and any remaining charges posted properly?				
Are all corrections controlled and balanced?				

AUDIT QUESTIONS	Yes ✔	No ✔	NA ✔	COMMENTS/ Followup Action
NIGHT AUDIT, continued				
Semi-automated and Manual Systems, continued				
Do all revenues balance to D card?				
Are traffic sheets reconciled to D card summary (or equivalent) by both the night auditor and the income auditor?				
Are procedures established and followed for recording and control of machine reset numbers?				
Does the night auditor run a trial balance?				
Automated systems				
Are all point-of-sale interfaces properly completed?				
Are housekeeping and other room reports reconciled to computer-generated reports?				
Are departmental totals reconciled, if necessary?				
Are all printed reports necessary?				
Are all printed reports properly distributed?				
BUDGETS				
Front Office				
Is the front office manager involved in departmental budget goals and the achievement of these goals?				
Are monthly operating statements reviewed and analyzed on a timely basis?				
Are recommendations for improvements outlined after review?				
Is the front office manager accountable for the budget variances?				
Is the front office manager accountable for the budgeting of "other expenses" charged to the front office?				
Are annual sales plans and operating budgets reviewed on a timely basis?				
Are planned front office capital expenditures included in the financial planning?				
Payroll Budget				
Have productivity statistics been developed and established by job classification?				
Are payroll costs percentages reviewed periodically?				
Are forecasting and controls used in establishing payroll budgets?				
EMERGENCIES				
Is the first aid kit stocked?				
Are front office employees familiar with emergency procedures for: fire?				
bomb threat?				
power failure?				
terrorist attack?				
serious illness, death?				
hurricane or earthquake or other natural disaster?				
Are emergency evacuation routes established for all rooms, public areas, and back-of-the-house areas?				

Registration Cards

UNIVERSITY INN
Registration Card

Folio #: _____

Name _____

Date _____

Street _____

City _____ State _____ Zip Code _____

Affiliation _____

Arrival Date	Room #	Rate	Clerk	Departure Date	Credit Card #

Remarks: _____
_____
_____

Money, jewels, and other valuable packages, must be placed in the safe in the office, otherwise the Management will not be responsible for any loss.

Cut along double lines   *Cut along double lines*

UNIVERSITY INN
Registration Card

Folio #: _____

Name _____

Date _____

Street _____

City _____ State _____ Zip Code _____

Affiliation _____

Arrival Date	Room #	Rate	Clerk	Departure Date	Credit Card #

Remarks: _____
_____
_____

Money, jewels, and other valuable packages, must be placed in the safe in the office, otherwise the Management will not be responsible for any loss.

UNIVERSITY INN
Registration Card

Folio #: _____

Date _____

Name _____

Street _____

City _____ State _____ Zip Code _____

Affiliation _____

Arrival Date	Room #	Rate	Clerk	Departure Date	Credit Card #

Remarks: _____

_____

_____

Money, jewels, and other valuable packages, must be placed in the safe in the office, otherwise the Management will not be responsible for any loss.

Cut along double lines   Cut along double lines

UNIVERSITY INN
Registration Card

Folio #: _____

Date _____

Name _____

Street _____

City _____ State _____ Zip Code _____

Affiliation _____

Arrival Date	Room #	Rate	Clerk	Departure Date	Credit Card #

Remarks: _____

_____

_____

Money, jewels, and other valuable packages, must be placed in the safe in the office, otherwise the Management will not be responsible for any loss.

UNIVERSITY INN
Registration Card

Folio #: _____

Date _____

Name _____

Street _____

City _____ State _____ Zip Code _____

Affiliation _____

Arrival Date	Room #	Rate	Clerk	Departure Date	Credit Card #

Remarks: _____
_____
_____

Money, jewels, and other valuable packages, must be placed in the safe in the office, otherwise the Management will not be responsible for any loss.

Cut along double lines   *Cut along double lines*

UNIVERSITY INN
Registration Card

Folio #: _____

Date _____

Name _____

Street _____

City _____ State _____ Zip Code _____

Affiliation _____

Arrival Date	Room #	Rate	Clerk	Departure Date	Credit Card #

Remarks: _____
_____
_____

Money, jewels, and other valuable packages, must be placed in the safe in the office, otherwise the Management will not be responsible for any loss.

UNIVERSITY INN
Registration Card

Folio #: _____

Date _____

Name _____

Street _____

City _____ State _____   Zip Code _____

Affiliation _____

Arrival Date	Room #	Rate	Clerk	Departure Date	Credit Card #

Remarks: _____
_____
_____

Money, jewels, and other valuable packages, must be placed in the safe in the office, otherwise the Management will not be responsible for any loss.

Cut along double lines   Cut along double lines

UNIVERSITY INN
Registration Card

Folio #: _____

Date _____

Name _____

Street _____

City _____ State _____   Zip Code _____

Affiliation _____

Arrival Date	Room #	Rate	Clerk	Departure Date	Credit Card #

Remarks: _____
_____
_____

Money, jewels, and other valuable packages, must be placed in the safe in the office, otherwise the Management will not be responsible for any loss.

UNIVERSITY INN
Registration Card

Folio #: _____

Date _____

Name _____

Street _____

City _____ State _____   Zip Code _____

Affiliation _____

Arrival Date	Room #	Rate	Clerk	Departure Date	Credit Card #

Remarks: _____
_____
_____

Money, jewels, and other valuable packages, must be placed in the safe in the office, otherwise the Management will not be responsible for any loss.

Cut along double lines　　　　　　　　　　　　　　　　　　　*Cut along double lines*

UNIVERSITY INN
Registration Card

Folio #: _____

Date _____

Name _____

Street _____

City _____ State _____   Zip Code _____

Affiliation _____

Arrival Date	Room #	Rate	Clerk	Departure Date	Credit Card #

Remarks: _____
_____
_____

Money, jewels, and other valuable packages, must be placed in the safe in the office, otherwise the Management will not be responsible for any loss.

UNIVERSITY INN
Registration Card

Folio #: _____

Name _____

Street _____

Date _____

City _____ State _____   Zip Code _____

Affiliation _____

Arrival Date	Room #	Rate	Clerk	Departure Date	Credit Card #

Remarks: _____
_____
_____

Money, jewels, and other valuable packages, must be placed in the safe in the office, otherwise the Management will not be responsible for any loss.

Cut along double lines   *Cut along double lines*

UNIVERSITY INN
Registration Card

Folio #: _____

Name _____

Street _____

Date _____

City _____ State _____   Zip Code _____

Affiliation _____

Arrival Date	Room #	Rate	Clerk	Departure Date	Credit Card #

Remarks: _____
_____
_____

Money, jewels, and other valuable packages, must be placed in the safe in the office, otherwise the Management will not be responsible for any loss.

UNIVERSITY INN
Registration Card

Folio #: _____

Date _____

Name _____

Street _____

City _____ State _____ Zip Code _____

Affiliation _____

Arrival Date	Room #	Rate	Clerk	Departure Date	Credit Card #

Remarks: _____
_____
_____

Money, jewels, and other valuable packages, must be placed in the safe in the office, otherwise the Management will not be responsible for any loss.

Cut along double lines   *Cut along double lines*

UNIVERSITY INN
Registration Card

Folio #: _____

Date _____

Name _____

Street _____

City _____ State _____ Zip Code _____

Affiliation _____

Arrival Date	Room #	Rate	Clerk	Departure Date	Credit Card #

Remarks: _____
_____
_____

Money, jewels, and other valuable packages, must be placed in the safe in the office, otherwise the Management will not be responsible for any loss.

UNIVERSITY INN
Registration Card

Folio #: _____

Name _____

Date _____

Street _____

City _____ State _____ Zip Code _____

Affiliation _____

Arrival Date	Room #	Rate	Clerk	Departure Date	Credit Card #

Remarks: _____
_____
_____

Money, jewels, and other valuable packages, must be placed in the safe in the office, otherwise the Management will not be responsible for any loss.

Cut along double lines   *Cut along double lines*

UNIVERSITY INN
Registration Card

Folio #: _____

Name _____

Date _____

Street _____

City _____ State _____ Zip Code _____

Affiliation _____

Arrival Date	Room #	Rate	Clerk	Departure Date	Credit Card #

Remarks: _____
_____
_____

Money, jewels, and other valuable packages, must be placed in the safe in the office, otherwise the Management will not be responsible for any loss.

Folios

UNIVERSITY INN

Folio #: _____

Guest's Name: _____   Room #: _____

Departure Date: _____   Today's Date: _____

ALL ACCOUNTS ARE DUE WHEN RENDERED

DATE							
FORWARD							
Room							
Tax							
Restaurant							
Beverages							
Telephone - Local							
Telephone - L.D.							
Laundry							
Valet							
Misc. Charges							
Cash Disbursements							
Transfer Debits							
TOTAL DEBITS							
Cash Received							
Allowances							
Transfer to City Ledger							
Transfer Credit							
TOTAL CREDITS							
BALANCE FORWARD							

Folio #: _____

UNIVERSITY INN

Guest's Name: _____   Room #: _____

Departure Date: _____   Today's Date: _____

ALL ACCOUNTS ARE DUE WHEN RENDERED

DATE							
FORWARD							
Room							
Tax							
Restaurant							
Beverages							
Telephone - Local							
Telephone - L.D.							
Laundry							
Valet							
Misc. Charges							
Cash Disbursements							
Transfer Debits							
TOTAL DEBITS							
Cash Received							
Allowances							
Transfer to City Ledger							
Transfer Credit							
TOTAL CREDITS							
BALANCE FORWARD							

UNIVERSITY INN

Guest's Name: _____   Room #: _____

Departure Date: _____   Today's Date: _____

ALL ACCOUNTS ARE DUE WHEN RENDERED

DATE							
FORWARD							
Room							
Tax							
Restaurant							
Beverages							
Telephone - Local							
Telephone - L.D.							
Laundry							
Valet							
Misc. Charges							
Cash Disbursements							
Transfer Debits							
TOTAL DEBITS							
Cash Received							
Allowances							
Transfer to City Ledger							
Transfer Credit							
TOTAL CREDITS							
BALANCE FORWARD							

UNIVERSITY INN

Guest's Name: _____   Room #: _____

Departure Date: _____   Today's Date: _____

ALL ACCOUNTS ARE DUE WHEN RENDERED

DATE							
FORWARD							
Room							
Tax							
Restaurant							
Beverages							
Telephone - Local							
Telephone - L.D.							
Laundry							
Valet							
Misc. Charges							
Cash Disbursements							
Transfer Debits							
TOTAL DEBITS							
Cash Received							
Allowances							
Transfer to City Ledger							
Transfer Credit							
TOTAL CREDITS							
BALANCE FORWARD							

Folio #: _____

UNIVERSITY INN

Guest's Name: _____   Room #: _____

Departure Date: _____   Today's Date: _____

ALL ACCOUNTS ARE DUE WHEN RENDERED

DATE							
FORWARD							
Room							
Tax							
Restaurant							
Beverages							
Telephone - Local							
Telephone - L.D.							
Laundry							
Valet							
Misc. Charges							
Cash Disbursements							
Transfer Debits							
TOTAL DEBITS							
Cash Received							
Allowances							
Transfer to City Ledger							
Transfer Credit							
TOTAL CREDITS							
BALANCE FORWARD							

UNIVERSITY INN

Guest's Name: _____   Room #: _____

Departure Date: _____   Today's Date: _____

ALL ACCOUNTS ARE DUE WHEN RENDERED

DATE							
FORWARD							
Room							
Tax							
Restaurant							
Beverages							
Telephone - Local							
Telephone - L.D.							
Laundry							
Valet							
Misc. Charges							
Cash Disbursements							
Transfer Debits							
TOTAL DEBITS							
Cash Received							
Allowances							
Transfer to City Ledger							
Transfer Credit							
TOTAL CREDITS							
BALANCE FORWARD							

UNIVERSITY INN

Guest's Name: _____   Room #: _____

Departure Date: _____   Today's Date: _____

ALL ACCOUNTS ARE DUE WHEN RENDERED

DATE							
FORWARD							
Room							
Tax							
Restaurant							
Beverages							
Telephone - Local							
Telephone - L.D.							
Laundry							
Valet							
Misc. Charges							
Cash Disbursements							
Transfer Debits							
TOTAL DEBITS							
Cash Received							
Allowances							
Transfer to City Ledger							
Transfer Credit							
TOTAL CREDITS							
BALANCE FORWARD							

UNIVERSITY INN

Folio #: _____

Guest's Name: _____   Room #: _____

Departure Date: _____   Today's Date: _____

ALL ACCOUNTS ARE DUE WHEN RENDERED

DATE							
FORWARD							
Room							
Tax							
Restaurant							
Beverages							
Telephone - Local							
Telephone - L.D.							
Laundry							
Valet							
Misc. Charges							
Cash Disbursements							
Transfer Debits							
TOTAL DEBITS							
Cash Received							
Allowances							
Transfer to City Ledger							
Transfer Credit							
TOTAL CREDITS							
BALANCE FORWARD							

Folio #: _____

UNIVERSITY INN

Guest's Name: _____   Room #: _____

Departure Date: _____   Today's Date: _____

ALL ACCOUNTS ARE DUE WHEN RENDERED

DATE							
FORWARD							
Room							
Tax							
Restaurant							
Beverages							
Telephone - Local							
Telephone - L.D.							
Laundry							
Valet							
Misc. Charges							
Cash Disbursements							
Transfer Debits							
TOTAL DEBITS							
Cash Received							
Allowances							
Transfer to City Ledger							
Transfer Credit							
TOTAL CREDITS							
BALANCE FORWARD							

Folio #: _____

UNIVERSITY INN

Guest's Name: _____ Room #: _____

Departure Date: _____ Today's Date: _____

ALL ACCOUNTS ARE DUE WHEN RENDERED

DATE							
FORWARD							
Room							
Tax							
Restaurant							
Beverages							
Telephone - Local							
Telephone - L.D.							
Laundry							
Valet							
Misc. Charges							
Cash Disbursements							
Transfer Debits							
TOTAL DEBITS							
Cash Received							
Allowances							
Transfer to City Ledger							
Transfer Credit							
TOTAL CREDITS							
BALANCE FORWARD							

UNIVERSITY INN

Folio #: _____

Guest's Name: _____   Room #: _____

Departure Date: _____   Today's Date: _____

ALL ACCOUNTS ARE DUE WHEN RENDERED

DATE							
FORWARD							
Room							
Tax							
Restaurant							
Beverages							
Telephone - Local							
Telephone - L.D.							
Laundry							
Valet							
Misc. Charges							
Cash Disbursements							
Transfer Debits							
TOTAL DEBITS							
Cash Received							
Allowances							
Transfer to City Ledger							
Transfer Credit							
TOTAL CREDITS							
BALANCE FORWARD							

UNIVERSITY INN

Folio #: _____

Guest's Name: _____   Room #: _____

Departure Date: _____   Today's Date: _____

ALL ACCOUNTS ARE DUE WHEN RENDERED

DATE							
FORWARD							
Room							
Tax							
Restaurant							
Beverages							
Telephone - Local							
Telephone - L.D.							
Laundry							
Valet							
Misc. Charges							
Cash Disbursements							
Transfer Debits							
TOTAL DEBITS							
Cash Received							
Allowances							
Transfer to City Ledger							
Transfer Credit							
TOTAL CREDITS							
BALANCE FORWARD							

UNIVERSITY INN

Guest's Name: _____   Room #: _____

Departure Date: _____   Today's Date: _____

ALL ACCOUNTS ARE DUE WHEN RENDERED

DATE							
FORWARD							
Room							
Tax							
Restaurant							
Beverages							
Telephone - Local							
Telephone - L.D.							
Laundry							
Valet							
Misc. Charges							
Cash Disbursements							
Transfer Debits							
TOTAL DEBITS							
Cash Received							
Allowances							
Transfer to City Ledger							
Transfer Credit							
TOTAL CREDITS							
BALANCE FORWARD							

UNIVERSITY INN

Folio #: _____

Guest's Name: _____   Room #: _____

Departure Date: _____   Today's Date: _____

ALL ACCOUNTS ARE DUE WHEN RENDERED

DATE							
FORWARD							
Room							
Tax							
Restaurant							
Beverages							
Telephone - Local							
Telephone - L.D.							
Laundry							
Valet							
Misc. Charges							
Cash Disbursements							
Transfer Debits							
TOTAL DEBITS							
Cash Received							
Allowances							
Transfer to City Ledger							
Transfer Credit							
TOTAL CREDITS							
BALANCE FORWARD							

UNIVERSITY INN

Folio #: _____

Guest's Name: _____   Room #: _____

Departure Date: _____   Today's Date: _____

ALL ACCOUNTS ARE DUE WHEN RENDERED

DATE							
FORWARD							
Room							
Tax							
Restaurant							
Beverages							
Telephone - Local							
Telephone - L.D.							
Laundry							
Valet							
Misc. Charges							
Cash Disbursements							
Transfer Debits							
TOTAL DEBITS							
Cash Received							
Allowances							
Transfer to City Ledger							
Transfer Credit							
TOTAL CREDITS							
BALANCE FORWARD							

UNIVERSITY INN

Guest's Name: _____   Room #: _____

Departure Date: _____   Today's Date: _____

ALL ACCOUNTS ARE DUE WHEN RENDERED

DATE							
FORWARD							
Room							
Tax							
Restaurant							
Beverages							
Telephone - Local							
Telephone - L.D.							
Laundry							
Valet							
Misc. Charges							
Cash Disbursements							
Transfer Debits							
TOTAL DEBITS							
Cash Received							
Allowances							
Transfer to City Ledger							
Transfer Credit							
TOTAL CREDITS							
BALANCE FORWARD							

UNIVERSITY INN

Folio #: _____

Guest's Name: _____   Room #: _____

Departure Date: _____   Today's Date: _____

ALL ACCOUNTS ARE DUE WHEN RENDERED

DATE							
FORWARD							
Room							
Tax							
Restaurant							
Beverages							
Telephone - Local							
Telephone - L.D.							
Laundry							
Valet							
Misc. Charges							
Cash Disbursements							
Transfer Debits							
TOTAL DEBITS							
Cash Received							
Allowances							
Transfer to City Ledger							
Transfer Credit							
TOTAL CREDITS							
BALANCE FORWARD							

UNIVERSITY INN

Guest's Name: _____   Room #: _____

Departure Date: _____   Today's Date: _____

ALL ACCOUNTS ARE DUE WHEN RENDERED

DATE							
FORWARD							
Room							
Tax							
Restaurant							
Beverages							
Telephone - Local							
Telephone - L.D.							
Laundry							
Valet							
Misc. Charges							
Cash Disbursements							
Transfer Debits							
TOTAL DEBITS							
Cash Received							
Allowances							
Transfer to City Ledger							
Transfer Credit							
TOTAL CREDITS							
BALANCE FORWARD							

Folio #: _____

UNIVERSITY INN

Guest's Name: _____   Room #: _____

Departure Date: _____   Today's Date: _____

ALL ACCOUNTS ARE DUE WHEN RENDERED

DATE							
FORWARD							
Room							
Tax							
Restaurant							
Beverages							
Telephone - Local							
Telephone - L.D.							
Laundry							
Valet							
Misc. Charges							
Cash Disbursements							
Transfer Debits							
TOTAL DEBITS							
Cash Received							
Allowances							
Transfer to City Ledger							
Transfer Credit							
TOTAL CREDITS							
BALANCE FORWARD							

UNIVERSITY INN
Folio Bucket Balance Sheet

Date: _____

This form takes the place of the calculator tape that would be run on folio balances.

Room Number		Folio Closing Balance
201		$
202		$
203		$
204		$
205		$
206		$
207		$
208		$
209		$
210		$
Total		$

UNIVERSITY INN
Folio Bucket Balance Sheet

Date: _____

This form takes the place of the calculator tape that would be run on folio balances.

Room Number		Folio Closing Balance
201		$
202		$
203		$
204		$
205		$
206		$
207		$
208		$
209		$
210		$
Total		$

UNIVERSITY INN
Folio Bucket Balance Sheet

Date: _____

This form takes the place of the calculator tape that would be run on folio balances.

Room Number		Folio Closing Balance
201		$
202		$
203		$
204		$
205		$
206		$
207		$
208		$
209		$
210		$
Total		$

RESTAURANT DEPARTMENT CONTROL SHEET

NAME: _____   **DATE:** _____

VOUCHER #	ROOM NO.	GUEST NAME	AMOUNT	MEMO
			$	
		Total Amount	$	

BEVERAGE DEPARTMENT CONTROL SHEET

NAME: _____   **DATE:** _____

VOUCHER #	ROOM NO.	GUEST NAME	AMOUNT	MEMO
			$	
		Total Amount	$	

RESTAURANT DEPARTMENT CONTROL SHEET

NAME: _____   DATE: _____

VOUCHER #	ROOM NO.	GUEST NAME	AMOUNT	MEMO
			$	
		Total Amount	$	

BEVERAGE DEPARTMENT CONTROL SHEET

NAME: _____   DATE: _____

VOUCHER #	ROOM NO.	GUEST NAME	AMOUNT	MEMO
			$	
		Total Amount	$	

RESTAURANT DEPARTMENT CONTROL SHEET

NAME: _____ **DATE:** _____

VOUCHER #	ROOM NO.	GUEST NAME	AMOUNT	MEMO
			$	
		Total Amount	$	

BEVERAGE DEPARTMENT CONTROL SHEET

NAME: _____ **DATE:** _____

VOUCHER #	ROOM NO.	GUEST NAME	AMOUNT	MEMO
			$	
		Total Amount	$	

LONG DISTANCE TELEPHONE CONTROL SHEET

NAME: _____   **DATE:** _____

VOUCHER #	ROOM NO.	GUEST NAME	AMOUNT	MEMO
			$	
		Total Amount	$	

LOCAL TELEPHONE CONTROL SHEET

NAME: _____   **DATE:** _____

VOUCHER #	ROOM NO.	GUEST NAME	AMOUNT	MEMO
			$	
		Total Amount	$	

LONG DISTANCE TELEPHONE CONTROL SHEET

NAME: _____   **DATE:** _____

VOUCHER #	ROOM NO.	GUEST NAME	AMOUNT	MEMO
			$	
		Total Amount	$	

LOCAL TELEPHONE CONTROL SHEET

NAME: _____   **DATE:** _____

VOUCHER #	ROOM NO.	GUEST NAME	AMOUNT	MEMO
			$	
		Total Amount	$	

133

LONG DISTANCE TELEPHONE CONTROL SHEET

NAME: _____   DATE: _____

VOUCHER #	ROOM NO.	GUEST NAME	AMOUNT	MEMO
			$	
		Total Amount	$	

LOCAL TELEPHONE CONTROL SHEET

NAME: _____   DATE: _____

VOUCHER #	ROOM NO.	GUEST NAME	AMOUNT	MEMO
			$	
		Total Amount	$	

ALLOWANCE CONTROL SHEET

NAME: _____   **DATE:** _____

VOUCHER #	ROOM NO.	GUEST NAME	AMOUNT	MEMO
			$	
		Total Amount	$	

LAUNDRY DEPARTMENT CONTROL SHEET

NAME: _____   **DATE:** _____

VOUCHER #	ROOM NO.	GUEST NAME	AMOUNT	MEMO
			$	
		Total Amount	$	

ALLOWANCE CONTROL SHEET

NAME: _____   DATE: _____

VOUCHER #	ROOM NO.	GUEST NAME	AMOUNT	MEMO
			$	
		Total Amount	$	

LAUNDRY DEPARTMENT CONTROL SHEET

NAME: _____   DATE: _____

VOUCHER #	ROOM NO.	GUEST NAME	AMOUNT	MEMO
			$	
		Total Amount	$	

Charge Vouchers

No. 1021

Charge

UNIVERSITY INN

_____ Department

Date: _____ 20___

Name

Date	Symbol	Amount	Room or Acct. No.

Do not write in above space

EXPLANATION

Signed by: _____

Cut along double lines.

No. 1022

Charge

UNIVERSITY INN

_____ Department

Date: _____ 20___

Name

Date	Symbol	Amount	Room or Acct. No.

Do not write in above space

EXPLANATION

Signed by: _____

Cut along double lines.

No. 1023

Charge

UNIVERSITY INN

_____ Department

Date: _____ 20___

Name

Date	Symbol	Amount	Room or Acct. No.

Do not write in above space

EXPLANATION

Signed by: _____

No. 1024

Charge

UNIVERSITY INN

_____ Department

Date: _____ 20___

Name

Date	Symbol	Amount	Room or Acct. No.

Do not write in above space

EXPLANATION

Signed by: _____

143

No. 1025

UNIVERSITY INN

Charge

_____ Department

Date: _____ 20____

Name

Room or Acct. No.

Date	Symbol	Amount

Do not write in above space

EXPLANATION

Signed by: _____

Cut along double lines.

No. 1026

UNIVERSITY INN

Charge

_____ Department

Date: _____ 20____

Name

Room or Acct. No.

Date	Symbol	Amount

Do not write in above space

EXPLANATION

Signed by: _____

Cut along double lines.

No. 1027

UNIVERSITY INN

Charge

_____ Department

Date: _____ 20____

Name

Room or Acct. No.

Date	Symbol	Amount

Do not write in above space

EXPLANATION

Signed by: _____

No. 1028

UNIVERSITY INN

Charge

_____ Department

Date: _____ 20____

Name

Room or Acct. No.

Date	Symbol	Amount

Do not write in above space

EXPLANATION

Signed by: _____

145

UNIVERSITY INN

Charge

_____ Department

Date: _____ 20 __

Name _____

Room or Acct. No. _____

Date	Symbol	Amount

Do not write in above space

EXPLANATION

Signed by: _____

Cut along double lines.

UNIVERSITY INN

Charge

_____ Department

Date: _____ 20 __

Name _____

Room or Acct. No. _____

Date	Symbol	Amount

Do not write in above space

EXPLANATION

Signed by: _____

Cut along double lines.

UNIVERSITY INN

Charge

_____ Department

Date: _____ 20 __

Name _____

Room or Acct. No. _____

Date	Symbol	Amount

Do not write in above space

EXPLANATION

Signed by: _____

UNIVERSITY INN

Charge

_____ Department

Date: _____ 20 __

Name _____

Room or Acct. No. _____

Date	Symbol	Amount

Do not write in above space

EXPLANATION

Signed by: _____

No. 1033

UNIVERSITY INN

Charge

_____ Department

Date: _____ 20 ___

Name _____

Room or Acct. No. _____

Date	Symbol	Amount

Do not write in above space

EXPLANATION

Signed by: _____

Cut along double lines.

No. 1034

UNIVERSITY INN

Charge

_____ Department

Date: _____ 20 ___

Name _____

Room or Acct. No. _____

Date	Symbol	Amount

Do not write in above space

EXPLANATION

Signed by: _____

Cut along double lines.

No. 1035

UNIVERSITY INN

Charge

_____ Department

Date: _____ 20 ___

Name _____

Room or Acct. No. _____

Date	Symbol	Amount

Do not write in above space

EXPLANATION

Signed by: _____

No. 1036

UNIVERSITY INN

Charge

_____ Department

Date: _____ 20 ___

Name _____

Room or Acct. No. _____

Date	Symbol	Amount

Do not write in above space

EXPLANATION

Signed by: _____

No. 1037

UNIVERSITY INN

Charge

_____ Department

Date: _____ 20 ___

Name _____

Room or Acct. No. _____

Date	Symbol	Amount

Do not write in above space

EXPLANATION _____

Signed by: _____

Cut along double lines.

No. 1038

UNIVERSITY INN

Charge

_____ Department

Date: _____ 20 ___

Name _____

Room or Acct. No. _____

Date	Symbol	Amount

Do not write in above space

EXPLANATION _____

Signed by: _____

Cut along double lines.

No. 1039

UNIVERSITY INN

Charge

_____ Department

Date: _____ 20 ___

Name _____

Room or Acct. No. _____

Date	Symbol	Amount

Do not write in above space

EXPLANATION _____

Signed by: _____

No. 1040

UNIVERSITY INN

Charge

_____ Department

Date: _____ 20 ___

Name _____

Room or Acct. No. _____

Date	Symbol	Amount

Do not write in above space

EXPLANATION _____

Signed by: _____

No. 1041

UNIVERSITY INN

Charge

Department ___

Date: ___ 20___

Name ___

Room or Acct. No. ___

Date	Symbol	Amount

Do not write in above space

EXPLANATION

Signed by: ___

Cut along double lines.

No. 1042

UNIVERSITY INN

Charge

Department ___

Date: ___ 20___

Name ___

Room or Acct. No. ___

Date	Symbol	Amount

Do not write in above space

EXPLANATION

Signed by: ___

Cut along double lines.

No. 1043

UNIVERSITY INN

Charge

Department ___

Date: ___ 20___

Name ___

Room or Acct. No. ___

Date	Symbol	Amount

Do not write in above space

EXPLANATION

Signed by: ___

No. 1044

UNIVERSITY INN

Charge

Department ___

Date: ___ 20___

Name ___

Room or Acct. No. ___

Date	Symbol	Amount

Do not write in above space

EXPLANATION

Signed by: ___

No. 1045

UNIVERSITY INN

Charge

Department

Date: _____ 20____

Name

Room or Acct. No.

Date	Symbol	Amount

Do not write in above space

EXPLANATION

Signed by: _____

Cut along double lines.

No. 1046

UNIVERSITY INN

Charge

Department

Date: _____ 20____

Name

Room or Acct. No.

Date	Symbol	Amount

Do not write in above space

EXPLANATION

Signed by: _____

Cut along double lines.

No. 1047

UNIVERSITY INN

Charge

Department

Date: _____ 20____

Name

Room or Acct. No.

Date	Symbol	Amount

Do not write in above space

EXPLANATION

Signed by: _____

No. 1048

UNIVERSITY INN

Charge

Department

Date: _____ 20____

Name

Room or Acct. No.

Date	Symbol	Amount

Do not write in above space

EXPLANATION

Signed by: _____

155

No. 1049

UNIVERSITY INN

Charge

Department

Date: _____ 20___

Room or Acct. No.

Name

Date	Symbol	Amount

Do not write in above space

EXPLANATION

Signed by: _____

Cut along double lines.

No. 1050

UNIVERSITY INN

Charge

Department

Date: _____ 20___

Room or Acct. No.

Name

Date	Symbol	Amount

Do not write in above space

EXPLANATION

Signed by: _____

Cut along double lines.

No. 1051

UNIVERSITY INN

Charge

Department

Date: _____ 20___

Room or Acct. No.

Name

Date	Symbol	Amount

Do not write in above space

EXPLANATION

Signed by: _____

No. 1052

UNIVERSITY INN

Charge

Department

Date: _____ 20___

Room or Acct. No.

Name

Date	Symbol	Amount

Do not write in above space

EXPLANATION

Signed by: _____

157

No. 1053

UNIVERSITY INN

Charge

_____ Department

Date: _____ 20

Room or Acct. No.

Name

Date	Symbol	Amount

Do not write in above space

EXPLANATION

Signed by: _____

Cut along double lines.

No. 1054

UNIVERSITY INN

Charge

_____ Department

Date: _____ 20

Room or Acct. No.

Name

Date	Symbol	Amount

Do not write in above space

EXPLANATION

Signed by: _____

Cut along double lines.

No. 1055

UNIVERSITY INN

Charge

_____ Department

Date: _____ 20

Room or Acct. No.

Name

Date	Symbol	Amount

Do not write in above space

EXPLANATION

Signed by: _____

No. 1056

UNIVERSITY INN

Charge

_____ Department

Date: _____ 20

Room or Acct. No.

Name

Date	Symbol	Amount

Do not write in above space

EXPLANATION

Signed by: _____

No. 1057

UNIVERSITY INN

Charge

_____ Department

Date: _____ 20__

Name

Room or Acct. No.

Date	Symbol	Amount

Do not write in above space

EXPLANATION

Signed by: _____

Cut along double lines.

No. 1059

UNIVERSITY INN

Charge

_____ Department

Date: _____ 20__

Name

Room or Acct. No.

Date	Symbol	Amount

Do not write in above space

EXPLANATION

Signed by: _____

No. 1058

UNIVERSITY INN

Charge

_____ Department

Date: _____ 20__

Name

Room or Acct. No.

Date	Symbol	Amount

Do not write in above space

EXPLANATION

Signed by: _____

Cut along double lines.

No. 1060

UNIVERSITY INN

Charge

_____ Department

Date: _____ 20__

Name

Room or Acct. No.

Date	Symbol	Amount

Do not write in above space

EXPLANATION

Signed by: _____

Credit Vouchers

No. 2021

UNIVERSITY INN

Credit

_____ Department

Date: _____ 20____

Name _____

Room or Acct. No. _____

Date	Symbol	Amount

Do not write in above space

EXPLANATION

Signed by: _____

Cut along double lines.

No. 2022

UNIVERSITY INN

Credit

_____ Department

Date: _____ 20____

Name _____

Room or Acct. No. _____

Date	Symbol	Amount

Do not write in above space

EXPLANATION

Signed by: _____

Cut along double lines.

No. 2023

UNIVERSITY INN

Credit

_____ Department

Date: _____ 20____

Name _____

Room or Acct. No. _____

Date	Symbol	Amount

Do not write in above space

EXPLANATION

Signed by: _____

No. 2024

UNIVERSITY INN

Credit

_____ Department

Date: _____ 20____

Name _____

Room or Acct. No. _____

Date	Symbol	Amount

Do not write in above space

EXPLANATION

Signed by: _____

No. 2029

UNIVERSITY INN

Credit

_____ Department

Date: _____ 20___

Name _____

Room or Acct. No. _____

Date	Symbol	Amount

Do not write in above space

EXPLANATION _____

Signed by: _____

Cut along double lines.

No. 2030

UNIVERSITY INN

Credit

_____ Department

Date: _____ 20___

Name _____

Room or Acct. No. _____

Date	Symbol	Amount

Do not write in above space

EXPLANATION _____

Signed by: _____

Cut along double lines.

No. 2031

UNIVERSITY INN

Credit

_____ Department

Date: _____ 20___

Name _____

Room or Acct. No. _____

Date	Symbol	Amount

Do not write in above space

EXPLANATION _____

Signed by: _____

No. 2032

UNIVERSITY INN

Credit

_____ Department

Date: _____ 20___

Name _____

Room or Acct. No. _____

Date	Symbol	Amount

Do not write in above space

EXPLANATION _____

Signed by: _____

No. 2033

UNIVERSITY INN

Credit

_____ Department

Date: _____ 20___

Name _____

Room or Acct. No. _____

Date	Symbol	Amount

Do not write in above space

EXPLANATION

Signed by: _____

Cut along double lines.

No. 2035

UNIVERSITY INN

Credit

_____ Department

Date: _____ 20___

Name _____

Room or Acct. No. _____

Date	Symbol	Amount

Do not write in above space

EXPLANATION

Signed by: _____

No. 2034

UNIVERSITY INN

Credit

_____ Department

Date: _____ 20___

Name _____

Room or Acct. No. _____

Date	Symbol	Amount

Do not write in above space

EXPLANATION

Signed by: _____

Cut along double lines.

No. 2036

UNIVERSITY INN

Credit

_____ Department

Date: _____ 20___

Name _____

Room or Acct. No. _____

Date	Symbol	Amount

Do not write in above space

EXPLANATION

Signed by: _____

No. 2037

UNIVERSITY INN

Credit

_____ Department

Name

Date: _____ 20

Room or Acct. No.

Date	Symbol	Amount

Do not write in above space

EXPLANATION

Signed by: _____

Cut along double lines.

No. 2038

UNIVERSITY INN

Credit

_____ Department

Name

Date: _____ 20

Room or Acct. No.

Date	Symbol	Amount

Do not write in above space

EXPLANATION

Signed by: _____

Cut along double lines.

No. 2039

UNIVERSITY INN

Credit

_____ Department

Name

Date: _____ 20

Room or Acct. No.

Date	Symbol	Amount

Do not write in above space

EXPLANATION

Signed by: _____

No. 2040

UNIVERSITY INN

Credit

_____ Department

Name

Date: _____ 20

Room or Acct. No.

Date	Symbol	Amount

Do not write in above space

EXPLANATION

Signed by: _____

No. 2041

Credit

Department

Date: _____ 20 ___

UNIVERSITY INN

Name

Room or Acct. No.

Date	Symbol	Amount

Do not write in above space

EXPLANATION

Signed by: _____

Cut along double lines.

No. 2042

Credit

Department

Date: _____ 20 ___

UNIVERSITY INN

Name

Room or Acct. No.

Date	Symbol	Amount

Do not write in above space

EXPLANATION

Signed by: _____

Cut along double lines.

No. 2043

Credit

Department

Date: _____ 20 ___

UNIVERSITY INN

Name

Room or Acct. No.

Date	Symbol	Amount

Do not write in above space

EXPLANATION

Signed by: _____

No. 2044

Credit

Department

Date: _____ 20 ___

UNIVERSITY INN

Name

Room or Acct. No.

Date	Symbol	Amount

Do not write in above space

EXPLANATION

Signed by: _____

No. 2045

UNIVERSITY INN

Credit

Department

Date: _____ 20__

Name _____

Room or Acct. No.

Date	Symbol	Amount

Do not write in above space

EXPLANATION

Signed by: _____

Cut along double lines.

No. 2046

UNIVERSITY INN

Credit

Department

Date: _____ 20__

Name _____

Room or Acct. No.

Date	Symbol	Amount

Do not write in above space

EXPLANATION

Signed by: _____

Cut along double lines.

No. 2047

UNIVERSITY INN

Credit

Department

Date: _____ 20__

Name _____

Room or Acct. No.

Date	Symbol	Amount

Do not write in above space

EXPLANATION

Signed by: _____

No. 2048

UNIVERSITY INN

Credit

Department

Date: _____ 20__

Name _____

Room or Acct. No.

Date	Symbol	Amount

Do not write in above space

EXPLANATION

Signed by: _____

No. 2049

UNIVERSITY INN

Credit

Department

Name
Date: _____ 20

Room or Acct. No.

Date	Symbol	Amount

Do not write in above space

EXPLANATION

Signed by:

Cut along double lines.

No. 2050

UNIVERSITY INN

Credit

Department

Name
Date: _____ 20

Room or Acct. No.

Date	Symbol	Amount

Do not write in above space

EXPLANATION

Signed by:

Cut along double lines.

No. 2051

UNIVERSITY INN

Credit

Department

Name
Date: _____ 20

Room or Acct. No.

Date	Symbol	Amount

Do not write in above space

EXPLANATION

Signed by:

No. 2052

UNIVERSITY INN

Credit

Department

Name
Date: _____ 20

Room or Acct. No.

Date	Symbol	Amount

Do not write in above space

EXPLANATION

Signed by:

No. 2053

UNIVERSITY INN

Credit

Department _____

Date: _____ 20 ___

Name _____

Room or Acct. No. _____

Date	Symbol	Amount

Do not write in above space

EXPLANATION

Signed by: _____

Cut along double lines.

No. 2054

UNIVERSITY INN

Credit

Department _____

Date: _____ 20 ___

Name _____

Room or Acct. No. _____

Date	Symbol	Amount

Do not write in above space

EXPLANATION

Signed by: _____

Cut along double lines.

No. 2055

UNIVERSITY INN

Credit

Department _____

Date: _____ 20 ___

Name _____

Room or Acct. No. _____

Date	Symbol	Amount

Do not write in above space

EXPLANATION

Signed by: _____

No. 2056

UNIVERSITY INN

Credit

Department _____

Date: _____ 20 ___

Name _____

Room or Acct. No. _____

Date	Symbol	Amount

Do not write in above space

EXPLANATION

Signed by: _____

No. 2057

UNIVERSITY INN

Credit

_____ Department

Name

Date: _____ 20

Room or Acct. No.

Date	Symbol	Amount

Do not write in above space

EXPLANATION

Signed by: _____

Cut along double lines.

No. 2058

UNIVERSITY INN

Credit

_____ Department

Name

Date: _____ 20

Room or Acct. No.

Date	Symbol	Amount

Do not write in above space

EXPLANATION

Signed by: _____

Cut along double lines.

No. 2059

UNIVERSITY INN

Credit

_____ Department

Name

Date: _____ 20

Room or Acct. No.

Date	Symbol	Amount

Do not write in above space

EXPLANATION

Signed by: _____

No. 2060

UNIVERSITY INN

Credit

_____ Department

Name

Date: _____ 20

Room or Acct. No.

Date	Symbol	Amount

Do not write in above space

EXPLANATION

Signed by: _____

Cash Turn-in Envelopes and Closing Bank Counts

UNIVERSITY INN
CASH TURN-IN ENVELOPE

Cashier Name:

Cashier Shift:

Date:

Bills:	$100.00	
	50.00	
	20.00	
	10.00	
	5.00	
	1.00	
Coins:	.50	
	.25	
	.10	
	.05	
	.01	
Checks and Vouchers		
Total Amount Enclosed		
– DUE BACK		
= DEPOSIT		
– DEPOSIT (from cash sheet)		
DIFFERENCE (over/short)		

UNIVERSITY INN
CLOSING BANK COUNT

Cashier Name:

Cashier Shift:

Date:

Bills:	$100.00	
	50.00	
	20.00	
	10.00	
	5.00	
	1.00	
Coins:	.50	
	.25	
	.10	
	.05	
	.01	
	Sub Total	
+	**Due Back**	
=	**TOTAL BANK**	

183

UNIVERSITY INN
CLOSING BANK COUNT

Cashier Name:

Cashier Shift:

Date:

Bills:	$100.00	
	50.00	
	20.00	
	10.00	
	5.00	
	1.00	
Coins:	.50	
	.25	
	.10	
	.05	
	.01	
	Sub Total	
+	**Due Back**	
=	**TOTAL BANK**	

UNIVERSITY INN
CASH TURN-IN ENVELOPE

Cashier Name:

Cashier Shift:

Date:

Bills:	$100.00	
	50.00	
	20.00	
	10.00	
	5.00	
	1.00	
Coins:	.50	
	.25	
	.10	
	.05	
	.01	
Checks and Vouchers		
Total Amount Enclosed		
– **DUE BACK**		
= **DEPOSIT**		
– DEPOSIT (from cash sheet)		
DIFFERENCE (over/short)		

185

UNIVERSITY INN
CLOSING BANK COUNT

Cashier Name:
Cashier Shift:
Date:

Bills:	$100.00		
	50.00		
	20.00		
	10.00		
	5.00		
	1.00		
Coins:	.50		
	.25		
	.10		
	.05		
	.01		
Sub Total			
+ Due Back			
= TOTAL BANK			

UNIVERSITY INN
CASH TURN-IN ENVELOPE

Cashier Name:
Cashier Shift:
Date:

Bills:	$100.00		
	50.00		
	20.00		
	10.00		
	5.00		
	1.00		
Coins:	.50		
	.25		
	.10		
	.05		
	.01		
Checks and Vouchers			
Total Amount Enclosed			
– DUE BACK			
= DEPOSIT			
– DEPOSIT (from cash sheet)			
DIFFERENCE (over/short)			

187

UNIVERSITY INN
CLOSING BANK COUNT

Cashier Name:	
Cashier Shift:	
Date:	

Bills:	$100.00	
	50.00	
	20.00	
	10.00	
	5.00	
	1.00	
Coins:	.50	
	.25	
	.10	
	.05	
	.01	
	Sub Total	
+	Due Back	
=	TOTAL BANK	

UNIVERSITY INN
CASH TURN-IN ENVELOPE

Cashier Name:	
Cashier Shift:	
Date:	

Bills:	$100.00	
	50.00	
	20.00	
	10.00	
	5.00	
	1.00	
Coins:	.50	
	.25	
	.10	
	.05	
	.01	
Checks and Vouchers		
	Total Amount Enclosed	
−	DUE BACK	
=	DEPOSIT	
− DEPOSIT (from cash sheet)		
DIFFERENCE (over/short)		

UNIVERSITY INN
FRONT OFFICE CASH SHEET

Date: _____

Cash Receipts

Room #	Name	Amount
Cash Receipts Total		

Cash Disbursements - Guests

Room #	Name	Item	Amount
Guest Disbursements Subtotal			

Cash Disbursements - House

House Disbursements Subtotal		

RECAPITULATION

	Total Receipts	
	Disbursements - Guests	
+	Disbursements - House	
−	Total Disbursements	
=	**Deposit**	

UNIVERSITY INN
FRONT OFFICE CASH SHEET

Date: _____

Cash Receipts			Cash Disbursements - Guests			
Room #	Name	Amount	Room #	Name	Item	Amount
			Guest Disbursements Subtotal			
			Cash Disbursements - House			
			House Disbursements Subtotal			
			RECAPITULATION			
				Total Receipts		
				Disbursements - Guests		
			+	Disbursements - House		
			−	Total Disbursements		
	Cash Receipts Total		=	**Deposit**		

UNIVERSITY INN
FRONT OFFICE CASH SHEET

Date: _____

Cash Receipts

Cash Disbursements - Guests

Room #	Name	Amount	Room #	Name	Item	Amount
			Guest Disbursements Subtotal			

Cash Disbursements - House

Room #	Name	Amount				
			House Disbursements Subtotal			

RECAPITULATION

		Amount
	Total Receipts	
	Disbursements - Guests	
+	Disbursements - House	
−	Total Disbursements	
Cash Receipts Total			**=**	**Deposit**		

195

Room and House Count Sheets

UNIVERSITY INN
ROOM AND HOUSE COUNT SHEET

Date: _____

Room Reconciliation

	No. of Rooms	No. of Persons	Room Value	Tax Value
Yesterday				
+ Arrivals				
= Total				
− Departures				
= **Today**				

Room Statistics

Rooms Available	
Rooms Occupied	
House Count	
Average Rate per Occupied Room	$
Average Rate per Guest	$
Percentage of Occupancy	%
Average Number of Guests per Room	

Usually prepared from room rack.

Room #	No. of Guests	Tax	Room Rate
201			
202			
203			
204			
205			
206			
207			
208			
209			
210			
TOTAL			

UNIVERSITY INN
ROOM AND HOUSE COUNT SHEET

Date: _____

Room Reconciliation

	No. of Rooms	No. of Persons	Room Value	Tax Value
Yesterday				
+ Arrivals				
= Total				
− Departures				
= Today				

Room Statistics

Rooms Available	
Rooms Occupied	
House Count	
Average Rate per Occupied Room	$
Average Rate per Guest	$
Percentage of Occupancy	%
Average Number of Guests per Room	

Usually prepared from room rack.

Room #	No. of Guests	Tax	Room Rate
201			
202			
203			
204			
205			
206			
207			
208			
209			
210			
TOTAL			

UNIVERSITY INN
ROOM AND HOUSE COUNT SHEET

Date: _____

Room Reconciliation

	No. of Rooms	No. of Persons	Room Value	Tax Value
Yesterday				
+ Arrivals				
= Total				
− Departures				
= **Today**				

Room Statistics

Rooms Available		
Rooms Occupied		
House Count		
Average Rate per Occupied Room	$	
Average Rate per Guest	$	
Percentage of Occupancy		%
Average Number of Guests per Room		

Usually prepared from room rack.

Room #	No. of Guests	Tax	Room Rate
201			
202			
203			
204			
205			
206			
207			
208			
209			
210			
TOTAL			

UNIVERSITY INN
ROOM AND HOUSE COUNT SHEET

Date: _____

Room Reconciliation

	No. of Rooms	No. of Persons	Room Value	Tax Value
Yesterday				
+ Arrivals				
= Total				
– Departures				
= **Today**				

Room Statistics

Rooms Available	
Rooms Occupied	
House Count	
Average Rate per Occupied Room	$
Average Rate per Guest	$
Percentage of Occupancy	%
Average Number of Guests per Room	

Usually prepared from room rack.

Room #	No. of Guests	Tax	Room Rate
201			
202			
203			
204			
205			
206			
207			
208			
209			
210			
TOTAL			

Daily Transcript Sheets

University Inn
Daily Transcript of Guest Ledger

Date: _____

1	2	3	4	5	6	7	8	9	10	11	12	13	14	15	16	17	18	19	20	21	22
Folio No.	Room No.	No. of Guests	Opening Balance DB (CR)	Room	Room Tax	Restau- rant	Bever- ages	Local Calls	Long Distance	Laundry	Valet	Misc. Charge	Cash Disburse.	Transfer Debit	Total Daily Charges	Cash Receipts	Allow- ances	Transfer to City Ledger	Transfer Credit	Total Credits	Closing Balance
Sub Total																					
DEPARTURES																					
Sub Total																					
GRAND TOTAL HOUSE																					

207

University Inn

Daily Transcript of Guest Ledger

Date: _____

1	2	3	4	5	6	7	8	9	10	11	12	13	14	15	16	17	18	19	20	21	22
Folio No.	Room No.	No. of Guests	Opening Balance DB (CR)	Room	Room Tax	Restau- rant	Bever- ages	Local Calls	Long Distance	Laundry	Valet	Misc. Charge	Cash Disburse.	Transfer Debit	Total Daily Charges	Cash Receipts	Allow- ances	Transfer to City Ledger	Transfer Credit	Total Credits	Closing Balance
Sub Total																					
DEPARTURES																					
Sub Total																					
GRAND TOTAL HOUSE																					

University Inn
Daily Transcript of Guest Ledger

Date: _____

1	2	3	4	5	6	7	8	9	10	11	12	13	14	15	16	17	18	19	20	21	22
Folio No.	Room No.	No. of Guests	Opening Balance DB (CR)	Room	Room Tax	Restau-rant	Bever-ages	Local Calls	Long Distance	Laundry	Valet	Misc. Charge	Cash Disburse.	Transfer Debit	Total Daily Charges	Cash Receipts	Allow-ances	Transfer to City Ledger	Transfer Credit	Total Credits	Closing Balance

Sub Total

DEPARTURES

Sub Total

GRAND TOTAL
HOUSE

University Inn
Daily Transcript of Guest Ledger

Date: _____

1	2	3	4	5	6	7	8	9	10	11	12	13	14	15	16	17	18	19	20	21	22
Folio No.	Room No.	No. of Guests	Opening Balance DB (CR)	Room	Room Tax	Restau- rant	Bever- ages	Local Calls	Long Distance	Laundry	Valet	Misc. Charge	Cash Disburse.	Transfer Debit	Total Daily Charges	Cash Receipts	Allow- ances	Transfer to City Ledger	Transfer Credit	Total Crecits	Closing Balance
Sub Total																					
DEPARTURES																					
Sub Total																					
GRAND TOTAL HOUSE																					

Notes

Notes

Notes

Notes